CW00732397

Towards the No̲o̲s̲p̲h̲e̲r̲e̲

Essays by

John M Dillon

Stephen R L Clark

Foreword by

Tim Addey

The Prometheus Trust

in association with

The Dublin Centre
for the Study of the Platonic Tradition

The Prometheus Trust
28 Petticoat Lane
Dilton Marsh
Westbury
Wiltshire, BA13 4DG

A registered charity no. 299628

Towards the Noosphere

John M Dillon
Stephen R L Clark

ISBN 978 1 898910 60 2

Published 2012

The moral rights of the authors have been asserted. All rights reserved. No part of this book may be used or reproduced in any manner without written permission, except in critical articles and reviews.

British Library Cataloguing-in-Publication Data.
A catalogue record for this book is available from the British Library.

Printed and bound in the UK by Biddles, part of the MPG Books Group, Bodmin and King's Lynn.

Contents

Cover: Drawing of an open spiral galaxy, face-on (possibly Messier 99), by R Dale, with acknowledgements to University of Cambridge, Institute of Astronomy Library.

The authors

John M Dillon is Regius Professor of Greek (Emeritus) in Trinity College Dublin, and a founder of the Dublin Centre for the Study of the Platonic Tradition. He was educated at Oxford and University of California at Berkeley, and specialises in the study of Plato and the Platonic tradition, on which he has written a number of books. Among his translations are works by Proclus, Iamblichus, Alcinous and many others.

Stephen R L Clark, formerly a Fellow of All Souls College, Oxford (1968-75), Lecturer in Moral Philosophy at the University of Glasgow (1974-83), and Professor of Philosophy at the University of Liverpool (1984-2009), is now retired from paid employment. He continues to manage an international e-list for philosophers, and to serve as Associate Editor of the *British Journal for the History of Philosophy*. His books include *Aristotle's Man* (1975), *The Moral Status of Animals* (1977), *From Athens to Jerusalem* (1984), *The Mysteries of Religion* (1986), *How to Live Forever* (1995), *Biology and Christian Ethics* (2000), *G K Chesterton: Thinking Backwards, Looking Forwards* (2006), *Understanding Faith* (2009), *Philosophical Futures* (2011) and *Ancient Mediterranean Philosophy* (2012). He is married to Prof Gillian Clark of Bristol University, with three adult children and one grandson. His chief current interests are in the philosophy of Plotinus, the understanding and treatment of non-human animals, philosophy of religion, and science fiction.

Foreword

Tim Addey

"The world," says Socrates in the *Phaedo*,[1] "is neither such a kind, nor such a magnitude as those who are accustomed to speak about it imagine. . ." Perhaps not much has changed in the two and a half thousand years since Plato wrote these words - humankind has regularly tried to comprehend the nature of the universe in which it lives, but so often falls short of a satisfactory understanding of it. At intervals our best minds describe the great cosmos and its limits, only to find a few generations – or even in a few short years – later, its known boundaries have been expanded, and our formulations of its fundamental laws need to be revised.

Running alongside this continuing failure is another: our inability to understand our own nature (and consequently our place within the greater whole) - hardly surprising, because the failure to understand either the macrocosm (the universe) or the microcosm (the human individual) reduces our capacity to understand the other. It is not an accident that the above words of Socrates - which precede a lengthy and profoundly symbolic description of "the true earth" - follow upon a careful examination of the nature of human soul, its relation to the body, and its immortality. The essays within this little book arise from the urgent question which John Dillon brings to our attention - "What is to be done?" Any intelligent response to this question must be qualified both by the nature of reality and that of our self.

Within the limitations of such a small book, we are given a glimpse by John Dillon and Stephen Clark of a number of views concerning the nature and possibilities of the universe in which we find

---

[1] *Phaedo*, 108c.

ourselves, starting from that of Plotinus' teaching in the third century C.E. and finishing with the work of some contemporary thinkers. And, of course, implicit within the various worldviews are a number of possible human destinies, ranging from a collapse of our own accidental and meaningless existence back into the nothingness from which our accidental and meaningless universe arose, to the very highest union with God – as a spark of light finding its way back into the super-intelligent fire from which it was generated. How are we to pick our way through the possibilities?

Perhaps our first task is to consider the Platonic supposition that the visible and temporal universe is an expression of an invisible and eternal paradigm: if this is a valid affirmation we can then explore what follows from it.

For those who are already convinced that the universe is a 'top-down' affair – that reality is unfolded from a single first principle through a series of powerful ideas or forms ultimately finding expression in temporal manifestation – this affirmation is a straight-forward one, albeit one that then requires its consequences to be thoroughly examined. However those who believe the reverse – that reality is built bottom-up, so to speak, with the more powerful and complex somehow arising from the simplicity and passivity of matter, the affirmation is contentious. A bottom-up universe seems to be the default position of the majority today (if, indeed the majority have a considered worldview): although our present civilisation has embraced materialistic concepts to an extent which is rare – perhaps unique – in human history, nevertheless underlying the superficial concepts to which so many claim to subscribe, there is still a foundation of what one might call Platonic non-materialism upon which all rests. When we observe physical phenomena, our natural reaction is to look for some law (or hierarchy of laws) which explain them: this means that we are looking into the invisible world for causes. Furthermore, we expect that once a law has been identified, it can be relied upon because *it will not change*: of course, part of our identification of a law includes an understanding of the place it holds in a greater system of laws, a system which limits the circumstances under which the law is effective. Thus when we find a law of nature apparently ceasing to have its normal effect, we do not shrug our shoulders and put it down to "magic" or "the will of God", we look for some more powerful over-riding law which can explain this cessation.

These laws – whether we call them natural, mathematical, metaphysical or divine – have certain characteristics, such as:

They are causal, and must pre-exist their effects.

They are unchanging and consequently they are unaffected by the existence, non-existence or the activities of their effects.

They can only be perceived by the mind, although their effects may be perceived by the senses, or our sensible instruments.

They have a reality outside of the flow of time, although many laws require the existence of time in order to become operable and manifest.

They are real, and are not the products of our thought, or indeed any other time-bound mind.

This is all very much a Platonic position, and the underlying Platonism of modern science – at least as regards physics and mathematics – is argued extensively and comprehensively in John Spencer's *The Eternal Law*.[2] Spencer points out that *logos*, or a rational, *incorporeal* cosmic order is not only fundamental to the structure of

---

[2] John H Spencer, *The Eternal Law: Ancient Greek Philosophy, Modern Physics and Ultimate Reality*, Param Media, 2012. p. 18

physical reality, but also to our understanding of that reality; he writes, "Although the logos is a nonphysical principle, it is similar in its function in the creation of the physical universe as the architectural plans are in the construction of a house. One essential aspect of the logos is expressed in the physical universe through the eternal mathematical law, similar to what Einstein would have called the abstract 'lawful structure'. This law must be beyond and prior to all physical phenomena, while being responsible for ordering all such phenomena. It is precisely because the universe is rational and ordered that we are able to do science in the first place."

An important point, I think, to be kept firmly in mind as the reader picks his or her way through the various possibilities our two essayists outline, is the question of the unchanging nature of the primary, non-physical cause(s) of our universe. If the entire scheme of manifested reality is born out of an eternal, unchanging and dynamic intelligible idea or paradigm, how can this cease to act as a cause? It is for this reason, that Plato in the *Timaeus*, says of the Demiurge (or the divine creator of the manifested universe) that, "while he was adorning and distributing the universe, he at the same time formed an *eternal* image flowing according to number, of eternity abiding in one; and which receives from us the appellation of time." Time as an eternal image of eternity is fundamental to Platonic cosmology, and as Dillon rightly says (page 8), such a concept requires time, and the universe of time, to be static (but perhaps better described as cyclic) – for a linear progression from a particular beginning to a definite end is not compatible with Plato's conception of timeless causes bringing about time-bound order.

The present consensus centred around the theory that the universe starts with a singular quasi-physical event, and that this event (the "big bang") forms what we understand to be space and time, seems, in its most unsophisticated interpretation, to run counter to the

Platonic version of reality. But it would be unwise to accept the theory in its primitive form – the consensus is by no means unanimous and is now increasingly questioned: see, for example, Steinhardt and Turok's cyclical cosmological theories outlined in their 2007 book, *Endless Universe*.[3] The idea that the manifested universe is one that goes through long periods of expansion and contraction is not only reflected in ancient Indian scriptures in which it is described as the exhalation and inhalation of the breath of Brahma,[4] but also, perhaps, in the *Republic's* speculations concerning great periods of fertility and sterility,[5] while Empedocles[6] has a dyadic cosmic cycle which alternates between the rulership of Love and Strife, so that "they never cease from continual interchange of places, thus far are they ever changeless in the cycle."

Whatever the full truth concerning our universe – and Clark's essay gives us a dazzling array of possibilities – we must ask ourselves how we fit into a scheme which has both an unchanging, eternal and immaterial element and an ever-changing, temporal and material element. In particular, we must consider the implications for beings such as ourselves who can contact both the unchanging and the changing elements: for we are not merely passive recipients of the causal energies of the unchanging order, but have the capacity to act within the structure of that order. All healthy human beings have an intrinsic ability to reason – that is to say, the ability to step between two or more immaterial principles, to link them, to draw further

---

[3] Steinhardt, P. J. and N. Turok, 2007. *Endless Universe: Beyond the Big Bang*, New York: Doubleday.

[4] Sometimes this expansion is called the 'day and night of Brahma': see, for example, Easwaran's translation of the Baghavad Gita, Shambhala Publications, Boston, 2005, p. 154.

[5] *Republic* 546a-d.

[6] Fr. 17, as given in Simplicius *Phys.* 158, 1.

immaterial conclusions, and, later, to apply such conclusions back down into the material world. We can, therefore, all energize about the intelligible order.

This kinship with the reality of the unchanging and immaterial order is in fact one of the proofs of our immortality offered by Socrates to his associates in the *Phaedo*.[7] It is no longer a given in our culture that we are essentially immortal (or indeed that we have a soul); nevertheless, when we turn to the question brought to our attention at the start of Dillon's essay – what are we to do? – we may do well to remember Aristotle's words[8] in the *Nicomachean Ethics*, "If happiness is activity in accordance with excellence, it is reasonable that it should be in accordance with the highest excellence; and this will be the best thing in us." He further affirms, that whether we consider this 'best thing' intellect or something else, "this activity is contemplative." So even if we cannot agree as to the exact nature of the universe, or our own nature, so long as we recognize that reality includes an unchanging order of things which shape the material world, and that our highest faculties are directed to this order of things, we may still arrive at the same conclusion as does Aristotle, that a human life which energizes about the intelligible order is truly happy.

But what does this mean? Is this activity of the contemplating self primarily that of discovery or invention? One fascinating theory presented here (from which this book takes its title) is that of the emerging 'noosphere' which, as envisaged by Père Pierre Teilhard de Chardin, suggests a parallel between the perceived emergence of life on earth with all its interconnections and organic wholeness, and that of an emerging intellectual sphere, also holistic and connected. It is

---

[7] *Phaedo*, 78b-85b, outlines what is termed 'the argument from similarity.'
[8] *Nicomachean Ethics*, book X, 1177a.

worthy of much consideration, and may well prompt the reader who attends to the various worldviews offered by both essays to wonder whether the noosphere is being constructed by our intellectual activity, or whether it already exists in the eternal realm, and we are moving back towards it. In other words, should we see it as being another element of the reductionist worldview, or, in some shape or form, another insight into the interaction between the unchanging purely immaterial order and the manifested order?

How we answer this question will have profound implications for our ethical life, because if we are the *creators* of the noosphere, then humankind must be seen as hierarchically above the noosphere – and, collectively, the measure of intellectual truth. On the other hand, if we are *discovering* the noosphere, then our place in the hierarchy of thinking beings is much less predetermined – and, further, humankind should be seen as being itself measured by the truths that underlie it. In the former case we can continue the modernist project which considers all human activities as means for shaping the manifested universe to our own ends; in the latter case we switch to the Platonic understanding of human activity as being directed towards a transformation of the self – a return to a divine likeness. The former view allows us to impose whatever we consider to be just upon the rest of the universe, while the latter means we must labour to know the Just in order that we ourselves become just and consequently more or less spontaneously act with justice.

The reader must decide for him or herself which of these two worldviews should inform the question *what are we to do?* However, both essayists here offer a similar practical response to this question: Clark writes, "Our best recourse is to do justice, to love mercy, and to remember that we owe our life and reason to powers beyond our control and present understanding." While Dillon says, "We do indeed, I think, have the opportunity to learn from our many errors, and move forward into a rational future, combining steady state on the material level, with ever-increasing progress on the intellectual and cultural level, but if we decline to take up that opportunity, by reason of the insensate greed or mere bovine stupidity of those that we allow to have power over us, then we will be swept away without pity or a second thought, or rather, we will be allowed to sweep ourselves away."

What these two essays offer to the thoughtful reader is a opening onto a field of speculation which should not be ignored: each of us directs a path through life based upon our supposed purposes and abilities – but unless these are seen in the wider context of humanity's purposes and powers, and beyond that, the universe's purposes and possibilities, our understanding of ourselves and our possible destinies will be hopelessly flawed. Of course given its limitations of size, this book could not possibly claim to be a comprehensive survey of its subject: but, as the Taoist sage once said, the journey of a thousand miles begins with a single step.

We are creatures who can look upon the stars and wonder: these essays invite us to do just that, and while some may hold that such vast speculations are beyond us, and that we should keep our eyes firmly on the ground upon which we tread, there is good reason to look, as far as we can, upon the whole of which we are a part, for as Lorenzo tells his beloved in the *Merchant of Venice*,

> . . .Look how the floor of heaven
> Is thick inlaid with patines of bright gold:
> There's not the smallest orb which thou behold'st
> But in his motion like an angel sings,
> Still quiring to the young-eyed cherubins;
> Such harmony is in immortal souls;
> But whilst this muddy vesture of decay
> Doth grossly close it in, we cannot hear it.

TOWARDS THE NOOSPHERE:

Plotinus, Origen, Teilhard de Chardin,

and the Striving for

a Rational World

John M Dillon

Preface

This pamphlet constitutes a component of the second trio of publications of the Centre for the Study of the Platonic Tradition, based in Trinity College, Dublin, but administered jointly by colleagues from University College Dublin, NUI-Maynooth, and All Hallows College, Drumcondra. As stated in the preface to my earlier pamphlet, the overall purpose of these short works is to bring some of the fruits of our deliberations to a wider public, and to stimulate a debate on the broad theme, 'What is to be Done?'. Our basic premiss is that modern western civilisation cannot continue on the lines that have been prevalent over the last hundred years or so, and especially in the last fifty years – the period of the reckless over-exploitation of oil and all other natural resources, renewable and otherwise, and must be brought back, by rational persuasion, reinforced by enforceable ordinances, to a state of mind which recognises the limitations inherent in our continued tenure of this planet.

Since this series was conceived, the 'crisis' envisaged in my earlier pamphlet has taken a dramatic turn for the worse. But perhaps in another way it is all for the best. Certainly, while prosperity – even apparent prosperity – was still rampant, forebodings about the future viability of our way of life were much more liable to fall on deaf ears. Now, for a space, we have time to reflect, and it will behoove us to use that time well. Hopefully, what will emerge will be a leaner, greener civilisation, more attentive to the needs and capacities of our environment, and to the call of the Spirit.

John M Dillon, December 2012

Towards the Noosphere

I

At the end of my last pamphlet, *Platonism and the World Crisis*,[9] I remarked that, although Plato was very much of a political philosopher, there were many other aspects of his thought from which one could draw useful lessons for the modern world, and that they might serve as matter for another occasion.

I feel now that this occasion has arisen, and that a discussion of Platonic metaphysics, viewed through the lenses of a selection of later thinkers, namely Plato's third-century C.E. follower Plotinus, Plotinus' older contemporary, the Christian Platonist Origen, and thirdly, the revolutionary modern Jesuit thinker, Père Pierre Teilhard de Chardin, may provide a source of inspiration for those in the modern world who, while no longer persuaded by the 'truths' of traditional religions, are dissatisfied with the alternative presented to them of a purely materialist, purposeless universe, and a materialistic, exploitative civilisation.

In my last pamphlet, I suggested reasons why the course being taken by the culture of liberal capitalism which dominates the West, and pervades much of the rest of the world, can only lead to disaster. But when we have emancipated ourselves from the dogmas of the Market, Growth, religious Truth, and the absolute autonomy of the individual, we are still left with the challenge of finding an alternative vision of the universe. Is the universe a random, accidental growth, in which the human race is merely an accidental bubble, soon to burst, or is there perhaps a cosmic structure out there,

---

[9] Prometheus Trust, 2010. Originally published by the Dublin Centre for the Study of the Platonic Tradition (2007)

directed by a divine intellect of some sort, which is concerned ultimately to lead all things to itself?

Let me set my cards on the table at the outset, and lay out in brief what I believe. Then I can proceed to try to justify it, and elaborate upon it, for the remainder of the work.

It seems to me, after many years of reading a wide variety of works, and reflecting intensively on what I have read, that the situation that we find ourselves in is more or less as follows. The realm of true reality is not this physical realm of existence, as would be the overwhelmingly prevailing view now in Western society, but rather a realm of immaterial, intelligible (and intelligent) reality, of which this physical level of existence is only a rather dim and confused shadow. To quote the poet Yeats:

> "Plato thought nature but a spume that plays
> Upon a ghostly paradigm of things..."[10]

Yeats was no philosopher, nor wished to be, but he did on occasion catch glimpses of deep insights into the truth of things, and of course possessed a marvellous facility for expressing those insights. I would thoroughly endorse his concept of the physical, natural realm as a mere 'spume' which forms on the outer surface, so to speak, upon the 'ghostly (in the German sense of *geistlich*, 'intellectual') paradigm', which is the realm of true being.

This realm of true being, I would maintain, is presided over by an Intelligence, or perhaps better, a Super-Intelligence (corresponding to the Neoplatonic One). One may call this 'God' for short, but I do not believe that this first principle constitutes anything like a personality, with likes and dislikes, or indeed specific preferences of any sort;

---

[10] From 'Among School Children', The Tower (1928).

rather it is an impersonal positive force, inducing (though without anything that can be, strictly speaking, described as forethought)[11] the production and sustenance, primarily of an intelligible universe, and secondarily of a physical, material one.

Why should it do this? Plato answers this question near the beginning of his *Timaeus* (29E), as follows: "He (sc. the Creator-God, or Demiurge) was good; and he wished all things to be, so far as possible, like himself." Timaeus' exposition in the *Timaeus* is, of course, couched in mythological terms, but Plato is putting his finger on a basic truth here – one that he maintained in conscious opposition to the mechanistic, purpose-free world-view of his contemporaries, the Atomists Leucippus and Democritus – that there is a force in the universe working, quietly and patiently, over millennia, and millennia of millennia,[12] to bring all creation to some kind of perfection.

What I wish to do on this occasion is to examine what forms this conviction takes in a series of thinkers dependent to a greater or lesser extent on Plato (though in the case of Teilhard, at least, not explicitly so). My two Christian authorities introduce into the theory a feature which in fact accords better with the insights derived from modern cosmology than does the essentially static system of Platonism, so I will give somewhat more attention to them. I will end, however, with some cautionary considerations, derived from a reading of the works of James Lovelock, another remarkable visionary of our time, who would not regard himself as either a Platonist or, I think, a Christian.

---

[11] As Plotinus is concerned to stress, in *Ennead* VI 7, 1.

[12] Plato could, admittedly, have had no inkling of the vast periods of time postulated by modern cosmic physics, but he did envisage at least millennia, and multiple world-cycles (cf. *Statesman* 272DE; *Laws* III 676Aff.).

II

First, however, Plotinus (204-269 C.E.). This is not the occasion to embark on a detailed exposition of Plotinus' life and works, but we do need to appreciate that, although a product of the Platonist tradition, and one who desired only to be a faithful expositor of Plato's thought, he was in fact in many ways a remarkably innovative figure.

First of all, he plainly gave thought to issues that had gone virtually unexamined, so far as we can see, throughout the previous Platonist tradition from Plato himself on.[13] Specifically, as regards the first principle, it is not clear from Plato's works whether he saw this entity as a providentially active Intellect (as is the case with the Demiurge of the *Timaeus*) or rather something higher, more transcendent, and possibly even supra-rational (as is the case with the Good of the *Republic*).[14] It is also by no means clear just how Plato saw this first principle acting on its creation, or why it should have been moved to create anything at all. All too often, when such issues are touched on, Plato takes refuge in mythical or poetical language, as instanced by *Timaeus* 29E quoted above. In this connection, it is less than clear whether we are to assume that there are externally-sourced limitations to the power of the first principle to achieve whatever its

---

[13] We have to recognize, however, that we are sadly restricted in our appreciation of many of the intervening figures, from the Old Academicians Speusippus and Xenocrates on, by reason of the virtually complete loss of their writings. Plotinus' immediate predecessor Numenius of Apamea is a particularly regrettable loss. The notable exception is Plutarch of Chaeronea, and even in his case many of his most serious philosophical works have perished.

[14] I leave aside the case of the One of the second part of the *Parmenides*, as, despite its importance as a first principle for later Platonists such as Plotinus, it is by no means clear how Plato himself intended it to be taken.

aims may be, as in the case of the postulated refractoriness of matter, or 'the Receptacle', in the *Timaeus* (cf. *Tim.* 52E-53A).

All these issues Plotinus ventures to address head-on, though without always solving them definitively. First of all, he is concerned to devise a formula which might explain why a totally transcendent, simple, and self-sufficient first principle should ever create anything at all. What he comes up with, in fact, is a creative adaptation of a principle propounded by Aristotle as something valid in the sphere of biology, that part of being a fully mature (that is to say, 'perfect', *teleios*) organism is that it should have the capacity (and the desire) to reproduce itelf. Plotinus transposes this to the cosmic level, and advances the principle that it is a condition of perfection in an entity that it should not remain wholly static, but generate something else. This action does not necessarily involve any element of deliberation or purposiveness; it is simply a process of natural 'overflowing'. There is a notable passage at the beginning of *Ennead* V 2, where Plotinus puts this well:

"The One, perfect because it seeks nothing, has nothing, and needs nothing, overflows, as it were (*hoion hypererrhyé*), and its superabundance makes it something other than itself. This, when it has come into being, turns back upon the One and is filled, and becomes Intellect, by working towards it. Its halt and turning towards the One constitutes Being, its gaze upon the One Intellect."

This presents us succinctly with a view of the beginning of the whole process, which involves not only an outflow from the higher principle, but a reversion of what flows out upon its source, which actually constitutes it as what it is – in this case Intellect. It is, further, a condition of this production that the generating principle produces something inferior to itself. This is simply a logical requirement. It is itself the best, so it cannot produce anything better than itself; nor yet can it produce something equal to itself, as there would then be no logical reason why the product should not have produced it – indeed, if it 'produced' something identical to itself, then nothing would have been produced at all! So it must generate what is in some sense 'worse' – in cosmic terms, something less unitary, less powerful, more diffuse. And this process must, with equal logical necessity, continue, down through Soul, Nature, and the physical world, to an ultimate level of diffuseness and powerlessness – where the product no longer has the power to revert upon its generating principle – and that is conventionally termed 'matter' (*hylé*).

This 'matter' serves as a substratum for the physical world, the world that we inhabit, and of which we are (insofar as we are bodily) a part, and it imposes severe limitations upon how perfect, or 'good', such a world can be; it can thus be regarded as in some sense 'evil'. Indeed, Plotinus often (e.g. in *Enn.* I 8, II 4, or III 6, 6-19) refers to it as such, for rhetorical purposes. But at the deepest level, Matter is generated by the One as a necessary part of a complete cosmos – the process could not have halted before all possibilities and levels of reality had been instantiated – and so, ultimately, to some minimal extent, Matter is 'good'. Its 'evil', in fact is tied to the fact that Plotinus regards it as ultimate Non-Being.

This whole process, however, Plotinus, as a good Platonist, regards as necessarily eternal. There was never a time when the One was not 'overflowing', when this cosmos was not created, and there will never be a time when it is no longer in place. The Platonist cosmos is not going anywhere; it is not progressing, and it is not degenerating. There may be ups and downs observable locally – droughts here, famines or floods there, increases and declines in population – but there can be no overall change of state. Certainly, this physical realm is subject to flux of every kind, but it is reciprocal flux; the physical world ebbs and flows, but it does not *progress*. It is up to the individual human being to work his or her way out of it.

III

This is in many ways an attractive scenario, but it is unfortunately not one which we can any longer rationally entertain. We know all too much now about the extent to which the universe as a whole is expanding and modifying (I hesitate to say 'developing'), and about what is happening to our own little planet in an obscure corner of that universe – not the rather ambiguous 'central' position that it occupied in the ancient world-view. A static, cyclic scenario will no longer do.

We need to turn now, therefore, to a different model, one that indeed owes much to the Platonist one, but which also introduces onto the scene an element that is radically different and new: the Idea of Progress. The figure on whom I wish to focus in this connection is the Alexandrian Church Father Origen, Plotinus' slightly older contemporary, whose creative blending of Christianity and Platonism, while fascinating to someone like myself, not surprisingly got him into fairly serious trouble, both in his own time and in later periods of antiquity.

I will confine myself for the present purpose to his major theoretical work, *On First Principles*, though he has much of interest to say elsewhere. Unfortunately for us, this work was so controversial that is has only come down to us in a rather sanitized Latin translation, by his long-time admirer Rufinus of Aquileia -- who was, however, most concerned that his hero should avoid condemnation for his more daring theories from such hard-nosed orthodox contemporaries as St. Jerome, and who consequently redrafted and watered down many controversial passages. Fortunately for us, however, Jerome was so annoyed by Rufinus' version of the work that he takes the trouble to specify, in a polemical critique, the *Letter to Avitus*, the doctrines of Origen to which he particularly objects. Jerome is certainly being polemical, but we have no reason to doubt that he is also being basically accurate[15], so that we have cause to be grateful to him for preserving some interesting doctrines.

I will not be concerned to explore all of these doctrines on this occasion, interesting though they are. What I want to do rather is to focus on his overriding vision, namely that this world is not something permanent, as was the Platonist assumption, but rather that it has a beginning and an end, or rather consummation, in which, to utilise a phrase from I Cor. 15:28 to which Origen was much devoted, "God will be all in all' (*ho theos panta en pasin*).

He turns to this question in the later chapters of Book I of the *De Principiis* (chs 5-8), and the first few of Book II (1-3). Like Plotinus, he is concerned, as a philosopher, with the mystery of why the physical world should have been created at all, and we, as rational souls, confined within it. As we have seen, Plotinus fixes on the notion that the very perfection of the One requires it to overflow, and to generate all the possible levels and varieties of creation. It still bothers him, however, as we can observe with particular vividness in his early treatise IV 8, 'On the Descent of the Soul into Bodies', how and why he, as a pure soul, should ever have got down here. He begins as follows:

"Often I have woken up out of the body to myself and have entered into myself, going out from all other things; I have seen a beauty wonderfully great and felt assurance that then most of all I belonged to the superior realm; I have actually lived the best life and come to identify with the divine; and set firm in it I have come to that supreme actuality, setting myself above all else in the realm of Intellect.

---

[15] And many of his allegations are confirmed by the later condemnation put out by the Emperor Justinian, in his *Letter to Mennas*.

Then, after that rest in the divine, when I have come down from Intellect to discursive reasoning (*logismos*), I am puzzled as to how I ever came down, and how my soul has come to be in the body, when it is what it has shown itself to be by itself, even when it is in the body." (1. 1-11, trans. Armstrong, slightly altered).

But despite such an exordium as this, Plotinus in this treatise is in a basically world-affirming mood. He is concerned to argue that, despite the untoward aspects of life on this plane of existence, the whole journey of the soul down here is an educational experience, and should be welcomed. Later, in ch. 5, he has this to say:

"So the soul, though it is divine and comes from above, and, though it is a god of the lowest rank, comes to this world by a spontaneous inclination (*rhopé autexousios*), its own power and the setting in order of what comes after it being the cause of its descent. If it extricates itself quickly,[16] it takes no harm by acquiring a knowledge of evil and coming to know the nature of wickedness (*kakia*), and manifesting its powers, making apparent works and activities which, if they had remained quiescent in the incorporeal realm, would have been no use, because they would never have come into actuality; and the soul would not have known the powers it had if they had not come out and been revealed." (5, 25-33, trans. Armstrong, slightly altered).

Here the idea is that the soul of the Sage will be perfected by its excursion into the material world, and will in turn have a beneficial influence on that world, through drawing it upwards to a greater degree of rationality. Origen is of course faced with explaining the

---

[16] This cannot, it seems to me, simply refer to dying young: that would not necessarily teach one anything very much. I take it rather that it refers to attaining a 'spiritual death' to the lures of this world, which constitutes a 'flight' (*phygé*), as advocated in Plato, *Theaet.* 176ab, enabling one to observe *kakia* without becoming polluted by it.

purposes of a much more personal divinity than the One of Plotinus, but he has a similar problem in explaining why this world had to come about, together with the whole host of beings both above us and below us, from the archangels Michael, Gabriel and Raphael above, down to Satan and his demons far below. In the last chapters on Book I, he explores the mystery of the descent of all created beings from a postulated state of unity with God in Christ, and he presents this as a series of 'falls' of varying degrees of seriousness, with the archangels and angels at the top, having 'fallen' only minimally, Satan and his evil angels, or devils, at the lower extreme, and ourselves somewhere in the middle, being previously existent pure souls who have fallen significantly, but who still have every opportunity of salvation.

For Origen, however, every creature, even Satan himself, possesses the ultimate possibility of salvation. This is a doctrine that got him into bad trouble, both in his own lifetime and in later ages, but it is of basic importance to his overall world-view. As he sees the situation, God has permitted the world to come into being, with all its levels of reality, to accommodate the free will of his creatures, all of whom (except for Christ himself) exhibit some degree or other of wilfulness (or what Plotinus would call 'daring', *tolma*), and so experience a 'fall' of some lesser or greater degree of seriousness.

Now this whole cosmic drama, though in one way the consequence of individual instances of wilfulness, from the Archangel Michael on down, is nonetheless a necessary process, in order that a cosmos be brought into being, and, by the working out of all possible concatenations of circumstance, a final consummation may be brought about which realises all the latent possibilities present in all souls. Since this mighty vision calls for even Satan himself working out his problems, and returning to the fold, a sadder and wiser soul (otherwise, Origen reasons, God's overall project would have to admit a degree of failure), he does not in fact envisage (though he is pretty reticent on this point, at least in Rufinus' sanitized version!) that all this will be worked through in one world-cycle, and therefore a succession of worlds must be postulated[17], but that does not affect the basic insight that this world is not static, but is going somewhere: there is a slow but steady drive towards order and rationalization, even if it may take a few cosmic rounds to reach its full realization.

Let us look at a few representative passages, to illustrate Origen's argumentative strategies. First, from Book I, ch. 6, 4:

"For if the heavens are to be 'changed'[18], assuredly that which is changed does not perish, and if 'the form of the world passes away', it is by no means an annihilation or destruction of their material substance that is shown to take place, but a kind of change of quality and transformation of appearance. Isaiah also, in declaring prophetically that 'there will be a new heaven and a new earth' (65: 17), undoubtedly suggests a similar view. For this renewal of heaven and earth, and this transmutation of the form of the present world, and this changing of the heavens will undoubtedly be prepared for those who are walking along that way which we have pointed out above, and are tending to that goal of happiness to which, it is said, even enemies themselves are to be subjected, and in which God is said to be 'all and in all' (I

---

[17] This is alleged, indignantly, by Jerome, in his *Letter to Avitus* 3-5, no doubt with justification. Rufinus prevaricates. Origen could be seen as borrowing the concept of a succession of similar or identical world-cycles from the Stoics, but a more immediate influence may be the Middle Platonist Severus, who also held to this view (Procl. *In Tim.* I 289, 7ff.).

[18] Origen is commenting upon Ps. 102:26: 'The heavens shall perish, but thou shalt remain; and they all shall grow old as a garment, and as a cloak thou shalt change them, as a garment shall be changed'; and upon I Cor. 7: 31: 'the form of this world shall pass away.'

Cor. 15: 28). And if any one imagine that at the end material, i.e., bodily, nature will be entirely destroyed, he cannot in any respect meet my view, how beings so numerous and powerful are able to live and to exist without bodies, since it is an attribute of the divine nature alone—i.e., of the Father, Son, and Holy Spirit—to exist without any material substance, and without partaking in any degree of a bodily adjunct.[19] Another, perhaps, may say that in the end every bodily substance will be so pure and refined as to be like the æther, and of a celestial purity and clearness. How things will be, however, is known with certainty to God alone, and to those who are His friends through Christ and the Holy Spirit." (trans. Crombie, slightly altered)

Here, in the context of a discussion of the consummation of the world, Origen seeks to adduce a number of his favourite authorities, including St. Paul and the Prophet Isaiah, in support of his theory that all of creation is being drawn upwards to a state of rarefied being, where we will still have bodies, but they will be of an aetherial nature. This, to anticipate slightly the final part of my paper, will in effect constitute a sort of 'noosphere'.

We find another passage relative to this a little further on, in the first chapter of Book II (1. 2):

"But God, by the ineffable skill of His wisdom, transforming and restoring all things, in whatever manner they are made, to some useful aim, and to the common advantage of all, recalls those very creatures which differed so much from each other in mental conformation to one agreement of labour and purpose; so that, although they are under the influence of different motives, they

---

[19] Origen seems to have wished to maintain that souls will not be left without some variety or other of body, that is to say, an aetherial body, even after their return to union with Christ.

nevertheless complete the fullness and perfection of one world, and the very variety of minds tends to one end of perfection. For it is one power which grasps and holds together all the diversity of the world, and leads the different movements towards one work, lest so immense an undertaking as that of the world should be dissolved by the dissensions of souls. And for this reason we think that God, the Father of all things, in order to ensure the salvation of all His creatures through the ineffable plan of His word and wisdom, so arranged each of these, that every spirit, whether soul or rational existence, however called, should not be compelled by force, against the liberty of his own will, to any other course than that to which the motives of his own mind led him (lest by so doing the power of exercising free-will should seem to be taken away, which certainly would produce a change in the nature of the being itself); and that the varying purposes of these would be suitably and usefully adapted to the harmony of one world, by some of them requiring help, and others being able to give it, and others again being the cause of struggle and contest to those who are making progress, amongst whom their diligence would be deemed more worthy of approval, and the place of rank obtained after victory be held with greater certainty, which should be established by the difficulties of the contest." (trans. Crombie).

We see here God presented as drawing all things to himself, not nullifying their individual free wills, but utilising them for his own superior purpose. Those who are able to 'give help' may be taken to be the Plotinian, or Origenian, sages, while certain others, it would seem, are put in our way just to try us, but all tend inexorably towards an ultimate fulfilment.

IV

But even this great vision of an ultimate *epistrophe*, or 'turning back', of all things, when "Christ will be all in all" does not quite get us to where I want to be. We, after all, know, or think we know, a vast deal more about the universe and its development than did either Plotinus or Origen, and any reasonable theory of human progress will have to accommodate itself to that. For that purpose, I wish now to adduce my third great witness, this time from the modern era, the Jesuit priest and distinguished palaeontologist, Pierre Teilhard de Chardin.

Père Teilhard had quite a vogue back in the 1950s and '60s, when his great work, *Le Phénomène Humain*, appeared (published first in French in 1955, and then in English translation, as *The Phenomenon of Man*, in 1959, though it was composed back in the 1930s), but his reputation nowadays seems somewhat dimmer. This, I think, is a pity, as, besides being a very noble figure, he seems to me to have enunciated important insights into the human condition, and the role of humans in the world.[20]

Teilhard had the difficulty, but also the opportunity, of being both a first-class palaeontologist and a convinced Catholic Christian – indeed a loyal member of the Jesuit Order. His problem was in a way not unlike that of Origen vis-à-vis the Platonist tradition, and he got into similar sorts of trouble during his lifetime, and to some extent after his death. His great work, indeed, was only published after his

---

[20] It has been put to me, by a Jewish friend, that Teilhard seems to take no account of such a phenomenon as the Holocaust in his optimistic view of human progress. In reply to that, one needs to bear in mind that he was actually composing his book in the mid-1930s, when Hitler was already an ominous presence, but there was little indication of what atrocities he was about to commit. One must also admit, though, I think, that Teilhard would have regarded even the Holocaust as something of a blip, rather than a reason for negating his overall vision.

death in 1955, through the benign subterfuge of bequeathing the manuscript to a friend, as he himself had been 'silenced' by the Curia, and prohibited from publicising his views,[21] and he respected that decision during his lifetime.

During his long years exploring the origins of humanity in the 1920s and '30s, mainly in China, Teilhard had come to formulate a sweeping vision of the trajectory being undertaken by Homo Sapiens from his origins as a deviant primate, perhaps up to two million years ago, spurred by the discoveries of tool-making and the use of fire, through the much more recent (c. 10.000 – 8000 B.C.) cultural developments of the Neolithic Era, such as pottery, farming, metallurgy, and ultimately the founding of cities (such as Jericho, Eridu or Nippur), down to the present age of high technology and incipient globalization, and beyond to an almost mystical vision of the future, which he characterizes as the Omega Point.

This vision seems to me to owe much to that of Origen, but Origen is not a figure that Teilhard ever mentions (whether he knew of him or not). On the philosophical side, he acknowledges a particular debt rather to Henri Bergson, and his concept of *évolution créatrice,* and to a series of creative geologists and biologists, such as Jean-Baptiste Lamarck and Eduard Suess (to whom he is actually indebted for the term 'biosphere'). Teilhard's world is one of ever-increasing systematic complexity, and, in parallel with that, a progressive growth in consciousness and self-consciousness. This, in his view, is leading mankind gradually, but at an ever-increasing speed, to advance from the biosphere, or level of life, to what Teilhard terms the 'noosphere', the level of mind, or consciousness.

To quote from p. 181 of the English edition:

---

[21] The Curia was particularly concerned, I believe, as to where Teilhard's theory left Original Sin.

"The biological change of state terminating in the awakening of thought does not represent merely a critical point that the individual or even the species must pass through. Vaster than that, it affects life itself in its organic totality, and consequently it marks a transformation affecting the state of the entire planet...

With and within this crisis of reflection, the next term in the series manifests itself. Psychogenesis has led to man. Now it effaces itself, relieved or absorbed by another and a higher function – the engendering and subsequent development of the mind, in one word *noogenesis*. When for the first time in a living creature instinct perceived itself in its own mirror, the whole world took a pace forward."

For Teilhard, the noosphere emerges through and is constituted by the interaction of the human mind with other minds, and first and foremost *with itself*. The noosphere has grown in step with the organization of the human mass in relation to itself as it populates the earth. As mankind organizes itself in more complex social networks, so the noosphere will grow to ever higher states of awareness. This is an extension of Teilhard's Law of Complexity/Consciousness, the law describing the nature of evolution in the universe. Teilhard argued that the noosphere is growing towards an even greater integration and unification, culminating in what he terms 'the Omega Point', which he saw as the goal of history. The goal of history, then, is an apex of thought or consciousness.

To quote again, this time from p. 259:

"It is only in the direction of hyper-reflection – that is to say, hyper-personalisation – that thought can extrapolate itself. Otherwise how could it garner our conquests which all are made in the field of what is reflected? At first sight we are all disconcerted by the association of an Ego with what is the All. The utter disproportion of the two terms seems flagrant, almost laughable. That is because we have not sufficiently meditated upon the three-fold property possessed by every consciousness: (i) of centring *everything* partially upon itself; (ii) of being able to centre itself upon itself *constantly;* and (iii) of being brought *more* by this very super-centration *into association with all the other centres* surrounding it. Are we not at every instant living the experience of a universe whose immensity, by the play of our senses and our reason, is gathered up more and more simply in each one of us? And in the establishment now proceeding through science and the philosophies of a collective human *Weltanschauung* in which every one of us cooperates and participates, are we not experiencing the first symptoms of an aggregation of a still higher order, the birth of some single centre from the convergent beams of millions of elementary centres dispersed over the surface of the thinking earth?"

For Teilhard, therefore, the Omega Point becomes the supreme level of complexity and consciousness, culminating, it would seem, in a sort of communal super-consciousness, where we will all think together as one. As it turns out, however, Omega is not only the *term* of the evolutionary process, but also the actual *cause* for the universe's growing in complexity and consciousness. In other words, the Omega Point exists as supremely complex and conscious, *independent* of the evolving universe. That is to say, the Omega Point is transcendent (cf. pp. 270-1).

In interpreting the universe this way, Teilhard feels that he is able to keep his concept of Omega within the orthodox views of the Christian God, who is transcendent (independent) of his creation. Indeed, he argues that the Omega Point resembles the Christian Logos, namely Christ, who draws all things into himself, and here he does, it seems to me, draw very close to Origen. For Origen, after all, the ultimate fulfillment of the universe was to be re-integrated into Christ, from whom it had initially emerged, by its 'fall'. Origen had, of course, no inkling of the spatio-temporal vastness or complexity of Teilhard's universe, but he does have the concept of a steady increase in the quotient of rationality, leading to the progressive creation of a 'noosphere'. Conversely, Teilhard's postulation of an 'Alpha' point, corresponding to the so-called 'Big Bang' of modern astro-physical theory, can serve as the equivalent of a 'fall', since the Origenian Fall (like the Plotinian fall of the soul presented in *Ennead* V 1) cannot properly be regarded as a moral failing, since it is clearly necessary for the achievement of the cosmos as a cosmos.

V

Now where does all this leave us? Well, I must confess to having spent some time in recent months reading the works of James Lovelock, particularly *Gaia: A New Look at Life on Earth,* and this has moved me to certain reflections., not entirely of an optimistic nature. The scenario that I have just sketched out here, arising from the speculations of Plotinus, Origen and Teilhard, is, on the whole, an optimistic one. There is arguably a force in the universe, an intellect of some sort, though not necessarily a 'personal' one, which is, broadly speaking, benignly disposed, in that it nudges, or draws, all living creation towards greater levels of complexity and consciousness. This happens, however over immense stretches of time, not without hiccups and setbacks, and not necessarily for the exclusive benefit of any one species, such as our own human one.

This scenario is supplemented, I think, interestingly by the theories of James Lovelock. For him, as an environmental biologist, the earth itself is a quasi-intelligent organism, which he terms Gaia, stimulated into action initially by a most provident combination of natural elements, unique to this solar system, but very probably by no means unique throughout the vastness of the universe as a whole, which has proved conducive to the generation of life-forms. Once this process got underway, however, he would argue that Gaia progressively takes over, striving for its preservation in the best possible state – what he terms *homoeostasis*, or 'steady state' – and favouring order over disorder. Lovelock, it must be said, has no notion of Teilhard's striving towards the noosphere, much less Omega Point, nor would he regard such speculations as part of his remit. All Gaia strives to do, in his view, is to preserve the balance of life. But it is in this connection that he transmits to us a serious warning, of which we would do well to take note.

The message is that Gaia does not actually need us, important though we might think ourselves to be; and indeed, if she ever came to the conclusion that we were causing serious disequilibrium in the system that she has established – that we were, in other words, not so much a natural species as a sort of virus – she would take steps to rid herself of us. This could arise in the form either of a temporary change in world climatic conditions which would make modern civilisation impossible to sustain, and/or the generation of killer diseases to which we had no antidotes, with the aim of either eliminating us altogether, or at least seriously cutting us down to size. We must bear in mind, after all, that we are not essential to Gaia; she would be just as happy with a species of interestingly mutated dandelions to take top billing in the drama of life. If we do not behave, we are expendable.

Now the case is different with the cosmic intellect of Origen and Teilhard (and of course that of Plotinus, though for him *Nous* is not concerned to lead the physical world in any direction, merely to maintain it). Here we have a force that is stimulative of ever-increasing complexity and rationality, and to that extent favouring the human race as a rational species; but even here we must not take anything for granted. The universe is a big place, and we flatter ourselves unduly if we imagine that we are the only project that the Cosmic Intellect has in train. We do indeed, I think, have the opportunity to learn from our many errors, and move forward into a rational future, combining a steady state on the material level, with ever-increasing progress on the intellectual and cultural level, but if we decline to take up that opportunity, by reason of the insensate greed or mere bovine stupidity of those that we allow to have power over us, then we will be swept away without pity or a second thought, or rather, we will be allowed to sweep ourselves away. There are, as I have suggested, many other promising projects such as our own available in the universe, and we will not be missed.

I composed my previous pamphlet, *Platonism and the World Crisis,* as I have said, at a time when there was not yet an overt economic and social crisis, merely a spiritual crisis. Now, just a few years later, we have a crisis on every front. We have, certainly, the means to make use of this crisis to rise to a new level of rationality, emancipating ourselves from dependence on non-renewable sources of energy, voluntarily limiting our population growth, striving to defuse irrational sources of conflict, religious and otherwise, and pressing on with important developments on the medical and biogenetic front that have been recently made. Indeed, it is heartening to reflect on how many potentially positive developments, anticipated, remarkably, by Teilhard -- though he can have had no notion of their details, writing as he was in the 1930s under the shadow of Hitler, Stalin, and a looming world war -- such as the United Nations, the EU, UNESCO, and a global concern for the environment, the Internet (itself dependent on the growth of the computer), the mobile phone – all developments with flaws, and the capacity to be used for evil purposes, but all potentially nudging us ever closer to the noosphere. So we do have the mechanisms in place on the basis of which to advance to a new level of global consciousness. But if we turn out to be incapable of doing that, I'm afraid there is no one up there that is going to take pity on us. As Plotinus remarks (III 2, 8. 38-9), " the harvest comes home not for praying, but for tilling."[22]

[22] He is here, it is reasonably suspected (by A.H. Armstrong and others), taking a bit of a dig at contemporary Christians; but his dictum is but a variant of the (much later) principle of (primarily Protestant) Christianity, 'God helps those who help themselves'.

SINGULAR AND PLURAL FUTURES

Stephen R L Clark

SINGULAR AND PLURAL FUTURES

Stephen R L Clark

Abstract

We cannot easily now feel the certainties that perhaps our predecessors enjoyed, whether about the cosmos or our own future. But perhaps we can still learn from the thoughts of earlier 'ages of uncertainty', in particular the Hellenistic Era. Speculation about that future, of our own species or society and of the universe, though more 'scientifically' informed, echoes or mirrors Hellenic and Hebraic speculation. Although mainstream thought is now professedly 'materialistic' and 'naturalistic', there are signs – in speculative cosmology and speculative futurology - that something closer to the older Platonic synthesis is being recommended. Neither the phenomenal worlds of our and other animal experience, nor the material world of interconnected bodies are ultimate realities: they are echoes or reflections of a mathematically discernible reality – and this too is not self-explanatory. In the words of Ernesto Cardenal, arguing from entirely theological premises: 'The realities we see are like shadows of all that is God. This whole world is made of shadows, shadows on the wall of a cave, as Plato said'. As Plato and his successors also said, we have some hope that we might leave the cave, and be united, or re-united, with 'the dance of immortal love'. Platonic myths and modern speculations form a strange match, despite their disparate origins, and Platonic thought can help to avoid mistakes in following up the modern story.

Thesis

Things don't have to be this way (whatever way that is), and very soon they won't be.

The same could truly have been said at any time in human history, but there have been times and places when grandparents could sensibly believe that they had good advice to give their grandchildren, that life was going on very much as usual, and that they had a broadly complete and accurate account of the world they lived in (only the details needed to be worked out[1]). Probably, they were deluded on all counts. Even when our ancestors were hunter-gatherers, after the ice retreated and all roads seemed open, they could not anticipate storms, earthquakes, droughts, the dying-off of species, and the arrival of half-familiar cousins. Even when our ancestors elected to settle down, to mark off village and household property, and build – with enormous labour – ceremonial centres for trade or worship or exogamy, the same hard rule applied. 'The things that men expect to happen do not happen. The unexpected, God makes possible' (a standard Euripidean tag, used in several plays: for

---

[1] Albert A.Michelson notoriously declared, in lectures at the Lowell Institute in 1899 (see *Light Waves and their Uses* (University of Chicago Press: Chicago 1903, pp.23-4)), that 'the more important fundamental laws and facts of physical science have all been discovered, and these are so firmly established that the possibility of their ever being supplanted in consequence of new discoveries is exceedingly remote'. This observation provides a good reason to suspect all similar claims, before and since: see Jonathan Schaffer 'Is There a Fundamental Level?' *Nous* 37.2003, pp.498-517: 'the history of science is littered with such speculations' (p.503). Schaffer's paper is an engaging attack – not without relevance to the present paper - on the belief that there is some one level, typically of 'elementary particles', that fully explains everything that happens (so that, strictly speaking, nothing is happening except the motion, as Democritus suggested, of atoms in the void: 'all else is by convention', DK68B9).

example, *Bacchae, Andromache* and *Medea*). This does not prevent our commonsensical assumption that we can count on things continuing as they are, and as we imagine that they have been. 'The commonest sense of all is that of men asleep, which they express by snoring'.[2]

The sober Englishman at the close of the nineteenth century could sit at his breakfast-table, decide between tea from Ceylon or coffee from Brazil, devour an egg from France with some Danish ham, or eat a New Zealand chop, wind up breakfast with a West Indian banana, glance at the latest telegrams from all the world, scrutinise the prices current of his geographically distributed investments in South Africa, Japan and Egypt, and tell the two children he had begotten (in place of his father's eight) that he thought the world changed very little. They must play cricket, keep their hair cut, go to the old school he had gone to, shirk the lessons he had shirked, learn a few scraps of Horace and Virgil and Homer for the confusion of cads, and all would be well with them.[3]

Wells' own half-serious efforts to imagine future possibilities, as also the efforts of science-fiction writers in the century since his day, were also of their time and place. They may at least have made particular possibilities rather less likely than they were. Their imagined futures, whether they thought them utopian or dystopic, were seen – correctly - as warnings rather than predictions. By imagining the likely effects, for example, of full-scale nuclear spasm, we have been guided away at least from that catastrophe, and now worry instead about the unintended effects of what had seemed merely benign improvements

---

[2] Henry David Thoreau *Walden*, ed. Stephen Fender (Oxford University Press: New York 1997), p.289 [ch.18].

[3] H.G.Wells *The World Set Free* (Collins: London 1956; 1st ed. 1914), p.35ff; see my 'Eradicating the Obvious': *Journal of Applied Philosophy* 8.1991, pp.121-5 (reprinted in *Philosophical Futures* (Peter Lang: Frankfurt 2011), pp.17-24).

in the quality and comfort of our lives. Wanting more than the world immediately provides – and driven by memories of those times and places where the world provided little – our ancestors cultivated plants and herded animals, devised new engineering skills, traded with other peoples and established rules and rulers to govern differences of taste and custom. Economies of scale and fear of peoples outside the law encouraged the growth of empires, the creation of specialized castes and economic classes. We chose – our ancestors chose, and we accept their choices – to cultivate new tastes, encourage material achievements and gather as much knowledge as we could of all the external changes that we half-remembered. Our time-frame, as well as our sense of space, expanded, so that it became half-rational to *plan* for our grandchildren's lives, and even for further futures that we will not see and cannot now imagine.

In his *Republic* Plato described how our ancestors settled down together, learning the peaceful rules of specialization and fair exchange, and how they found it necessary to protect themselves against each other and against invaders, as well as planning invasions of their own in pursuit of little luxuries. 'The city of pigs' gave way to the fevered city, and the prospect of unending war to safeguard imperial ambitions, and the comfort of the protected classes[4]. His proffered solution to the fever was to inculcate – at least in those with the energy and wit to govern his imagined city – a devotion to the 'good' (or at least the peace) of the whole city. The rulers were to be bred, trained and educated to that goal, and tested almost to destruction so that only those truly immune to bribery and threat could ever hold authority. He sadly acknowledged that even such rulers could not long be preserved against corruption. The beauty of

[4] On the reasons why Plato did *not* think pigs ridiculous, see my 'Herds of Free Bipeds' in C.Rowe, ed., *Reading the Statesman: proceedings of the Third Symposium Platonicum* (Academia Verlag: Sankt Augustin 1995), pp.236-52 (reprinted in *The Political Animal* (Routledge: London 1999), pp.134-54).

an ordered city, keeping within its literal and moral bounds and threatening none, was an ideal that would mutate: the rulers would begin to favour their own stock, their own achievements, their own comforts over the good of all. They would long since have lost sight of Real Beauty when their city turned into yet another imperial city, no longer – if it ever was – a 'city on a hill', a light for all nations. John Winthrop's exhortation to his fellow colonists would have had some support from Plato.

> Now the onely way to avoyde this shipwracke and to provide for our posterity is to followe the Counsell of Micah [*Micah* 6.8], to doe Justly, to love mercy, to walke humbly with our God, for this end, wee must be knitt together in this worke as one man, wee must entertaine each other in brotherly Affeccion, wee must be willing to abridge our selves of our superfluities, for the supply of others necessities, wee must uphold a familiar Commerce together in all meekenes, gentlenes, patience and liberallity, wee must delight in eache other, make others Condicions our owne, rejoyce together, mourne together, labour, and suffer together, allwayes haveing before our eyes our Commission and Community in the worke, our Community as members of the same body, soe shall wee keepe the unitie of the spirit in the bond of peace, the Lord will be our God and delight to dwell among us, as his owne people. ... Hee shall make us a prayse and glory, that men shall say of succeeding plantacions: the lord make it like that of New England: for wee must Consider that wee shall be as a Citty upon a Hill, the eies of all people are uppon us [*Matthew* 5.14-16]; soe that if wee shall deale falsely with our god in this worke wee have undertaken and soe cause him to withdrawe his present help from us, wee shall be made a story and a byword through the world ...till wee be consumed out of the good land whether wee are going: And to shutt upp this discourse with that exhortacion of Moses that faithfull servant of the Lord in his last farewell to Israell [*Deuteronomy* 30]. Beloved there is now sett

before us life, and good, deathe and evill in that wee are Commaunded this day to love the Lord our God, and to love one another to walke in his wayes and to keepe his Commaundements and his Ordinance, and his lawes, and the Articles of our Covenant with him that wee may live and be multiplyed, and that the Lord our God may blesse us in the land whether wee goe to possesse it: But if our heartes shall turne away soe that wee will not obey, but shall be seduced and worshipp other Gods our pleasures, and proffitts, and serve them, it is propounded unto us this day, wee shall surely perishe out of the good Land whether wee passe over this vast Sea to possesse it; Therefore lett us choose life, that wee, and our Seede, may live; by obeyeing his voyce, and cleaveing to him, for hee is our life, and our prosperity.[5]

That phrase – 'a City on the Hill' - has echoed through later American rhetoric, but has often seemed rather to promote imperial self-satisfaction than warn against error – just as Rudyard Kipling's 'Recessional' (1897) has been interpreted – in absolute contradiction of its author's message – as an imperialistic tract.[6] The actual conduct of the Puritan colonists towards the original inhabitants of the lands they seized was modelled – in their eyes – on the conduct of the invading Hebrews toward the inhabitants of Canaan, without even the sad excuse that the natives engaged in religious and moral practices that we too would condemn. As George Berkeley observed, 'our first Planters imagined they had a right to treat Indians on the

[5] Taken from http://www.mtholyoke.edu/acad/intrel/winthrop.htm (accessed 21st April 2012). There is a balanced account of Winthrop in Francis J. Bremer *John Winthrop: America's Forgotten Founding Father* (OUP: New York 2003).

[6] See Rudyard Kipling *Something of Myself* (Wordsworth: Ware 2008) p.78 (1st published 1920): 'It was more in the nature of a *nuzzur-wattu* (an averter of the Evil Eye)'.

foot of Canaanites or Amalekites'[7]. Because the native inhabitants had not 'improved' the land (or so the colonists supposed) they had no title to it. Sadly again, *Greek* colonies across the Mediterranean were similarly disrespectful of indigenous peoples, supposing them 'barbarians' without the sense of 'justice' that Zeus had ordained for real people like the Greeks[8]. Winthrop's insistence on the virtues of community, like Plato's, seem to be sustained by exiling or executing any heretics who challenged one particular account of 'justice'. It would be a romantic error to imagine that such exiles were always themselves more 'liberal' or more compassionate, but we may suspect that a better sense of justice has arisen among those who did not so eagerly insist that *they* were God's Elect, even if only on probation! Both the lives of sensual enjoyment and of honourable achievement may give excuses for mere *pleonexia*, which is 'wanting more' at whatever cost. The life of awestruck contemplation, *theoria*, was the philosophers' answer, delighting in the beauty of reality – but that too has its perversions.

Our problem remains. We do not know what will happen next. We do not know what Change is heading our way from the heavens: what sudden change in solar radiation, what stellar explosion, what hidden asteroid, what collapse of the present 'false vacuum' into a

---

[7] George Berkeley 'Society for the Propagation of the Gospel Anniversary Sermon: *Collected Works*, edds., A.A.Luce & T.E.Jessop, vol.7 (Thomas Nelson: London 1955), p.122.

[8] Hesiod *Works and Days* 1.275ff: 'the son of Cronos [that is, Zeus] has ordained this law for men, that fishes and beasts and winged fowls should devour one another, for right [*dike*] is not in them; but to mankind he gave right which proves far the best'. 'Mankind', historically, has almost always meant 'our tribe', but the very term presents the potential for a wider expansion of our concern (inadequate as it may be).

lower energy state[9], nor even whether the extraterrestrials which are probably Out There somewhere will decide to intervene[10]. Even such changes as are driven by merely human, social and political processes are bound to be unexpected. Speculative extrapolation of current trends, or what we are assured are current trends, has not been very successful in the past. William Gibson's short story, 'The Gernsback Continuum', imagines what future might have been if the founding father of science fiction, Hugo Gernsback, had had his way: 'it had all the sinister fruitiness of a Hitler Youth propaganda'.[11] Gibson himself imagined 'cyberspace' into being before the World Wide Web was established, and before there were any tools to create the 'virtual realities' and 'simulations' that now seem commonplace to a growing

[9] Any such lower-energy vacuum state, if it occurred anywhere, would expand at the speed of light – and so eliminate us all without any warning! 'The possibility that we are living in a false [unstable] vacuum has never been a cheering one to contemplate. Vacuum decay is the ultimate ecological catastrophe; in a new vacuum there are new constants of nature; after vacuum decay, not only is life as we know it impossible, so is chemistry as we know it. However, one could always draw stoic comfort from the possibility that perhaps in the course of time the new vacuum would sustain, if not life as we know it, at least some structures capable of knowing joy. This possibility has now been eliminated': Sidney Coleman & Frank De Luccia 'Gravitational effects on and of vacuum decay': *Physical Review D* 21.1980, pp.3305–3315: p.3314. The more one discovers about the universe the less likely our existence seems (on which more below).

[10] See John Leslie *The End of the World: The Science and Ethics of Human Extinction* (Routledge: London 1996) for a summary of these and other possibilities, in the light of the Doomsday Argument that we are very likely to be in the largest generation of humanity (and so probably near its end). See also my 'Deep Time: does it matter?' in George Ellis, ed., *The Far-Future Universe* (Templeton Foundation Press: Radnor, Pennsylvania 2002), pp.177-95.

[11] William Gibson *Burning Chrome* (Grafton Books: London 1988), pp.36-50 (first published 1980).

generation[12]. Earlier SF writers who also imagined the development of the computer industry, and 'artificial intelligence', did not anticipate the effects of 'Moore's Law' (that computing power doubles every two years – or slightly less[13]). Both Gibson and his predecessors may have helped inspire creative engineers to produce the things they prophesied, but it is likely that their inspiration will one day seem as old-fashioned and faintly disagreeable as Gernsback's! In the Fifties SF writers were, roughly, divided between those who warned of the effects of nuclear spasm, and those who seemed to relish the idea that there would one day be a Universal Computer, 'Multivac' or simply 'the Machines', to direct our economic and political affairs (often without letting anyone know that this is what It was doing, and without questioning the inchoate goals it had been set)[14]. We have experienced – so far – neither of

[12] See William Gibson *Neuromancer* (Gollancz: London 1984) and its sequels, *Count Zero* (1986) and *Mona Lisa Overdrive* (1988).

[13] See Gordon E.Moore 'Cramming more components onto integrated circuits' *Electronics* 38.8, 19th April 1965. In its original form the rule was simply that the number of transistors that could be placed on an integrated circuit for the same cost would double roughly every two years ('the complexity for minimum component costs has increased at a rate of roughly a factor of two per year'). It quickly became a more general prediction, about the doubling of computer power, and despite frequent predictions that it would cease to apply quite soon, it has continued to be true. Some futurists have inferred that our artefacts will soon be faster, smarter and more self-aware than we are: see Ray Kurzweil *The Singularity is Near: when humans transcend biology* (Duckworth: London 2005).

[14] See, for example, Isaac Asimov 'The Evitable Conflict' (1950): *The Complete Robot* (Granada: London 1982), pp.546-74. The so-called Three Laws of Robotics that Asimov devised to encapsulate a moral system of sorts for his imagined robots were never satisfactory, and later writers have drawn out their genocidal and totalitarian implications: see, for example, Gregory Benford *Foundation's Fear* (HarperCollins: New York 1997).

these futures, and may not experience the laissez-faire capitalist future (dominated by criminal gangs) that Gibson imagined – nor yet the Singularity when computing power wholly transcends our understanding of what the networked computers are doing, and why (to which imagined future I shall return).

We do not know what will happen, and so we cannot sensibly prepare for any particular future. The best we can do is devise, restore or hang on to some sense of beauty, justice, mercy - and humility (especially in the light of our obvious past failures). Maybe our successors – who may not be our descendants – will have reverted to nomadic life on a planet wracked by storms and shifting populations. Maybe they will be plugged in to some successor of the World Wide Web, and every individual have access to information, intelligence – and power - beyond what we can imagine. Maybe they will thereby fulfil the fantasy found in many 20th century writers (and not only Chardin), of being taken up into a larger, wiser whole[15]. Maybe they will have expanded out into the solar system, or the galactic spiral, and be indulging whatever special fancies each strand of human or post-human life may have. Whatever life they are living they will need virtues of a familiar kind: courage, courtesy, self-

[15] Olaf Stapledon *Last and First Men* (Penguin: Harmondsworth 1972; 1st published 1930) and *Star Maker* (Methuen: London 1937); Arthur C.Clarke *Childhood's End* (Sidgwick & Jackson: London 1954); Robert Charles Wilson *The Harvest* (Bantam: New York 1992). See John Connolly 'A Progressive End: Arthur C.Clarke & Teilhard de Chardin': *Foundation* 61.1994, pp.66-76: Connolly suggests that – despite Clarke's denials – Chardin's ideas were sufficiently widespread, even before their publication, that they may have influenced Clarke. This may be so, but Stapledon seems to be a likelier, and acknowledged, source. Frederik Pohl & Jack Williamson took a distinctly more hostile view in *Land's End* (Tor Books: New York 1989): there 'the Eternal' – modelled either on Clarke's Overmind or Lovecraft's Cthulhu - is a monster which, by absorbing all terrestrial life, would put an end to it.

possession, justice, compassion and 'good sense'. Perhaps they have as much chance of achieving this as any human generation – but perhaps no greater chance. It is also horridly possible that our species will be divided, and our descendants be either prey or predator, as Wells imagined. It is possible that we shall find the heavens are already occupied, by beings with little sympathy for us. And also possible that we will have no successors.

Antithesis

Things don't have to be this way – or else perhaps they do.

Most of us have accepted that it is through 'science' that we shall obtain the knowledge and the power that we suppose our predecessors wanted, even if we are unhappy with the inference that anything like Multivac should control our lives by calculating the 'most efficient' route to a utilitarian goal (the greatest available satisfaction of the greatest number). We do therefore have some duty to understand what 'science' is currently suggesting. Mainstream scientific opinion has for some centuries been Stoic in its inspiration. There are finitely many bodies, undergoing finitely many changes, and what is happening at any given point in space or time is all that possibly can. History, whether cosmic or terrestrial, repeats itself 'forever', whether or not there is a period, the Conflagration or the Big Crunch, when every lesser body is gathered back into the cosmic Singularity. An ideal intelligence would be able to work out the whole world's history and geography from detailed study of a falling leaf, since every feature of that leaf's fall is linked to everything else that happens, everywhere and every when (except that even an ideal intelligence could not know every relevant property of its fall[16]). An ideal intelligence would at least understand the Formula of All Things, and know that it couldn't be otherwise: it would 'know the Mind of God', in Hawking's misleading phrase[17]. Not only is our history fixed, but nothing of it is owed to 'chance' or arbitrary decision. It follows – though hardly any of us can manage this conversion – that we cannot sanely resent any feature of the world, however harsh it seems: to wish it otherwise is not merely to wish the whole world to be unimaginably different, but to wish the whole world away. Epictetus imagines Zeus instructing him that his only 'freedom' is deciding how to feel about the way things are and must be[18] – but of course there is no real possibility that Epictetus could feel otherwise than he does.

This has been the scientific hope, even when the scientists themselves continued to act as if they were free agents with a real duty to discover and to tell the truth, and some chance of doing so (how else,

[16] Partly because the attempt to discover those properties must alter them, and partly because there is good reason to doubt the application of the Law of Non-Contradiction at the quantum level (so that an elementary particle may be in several different, apparently distinct, states at the same time) and hence good reason to suspect that not all these different states are subsumed into a single macroscopic event. Maybe the leaf falls all the ways it can – on which I shall more to say hereafter.

[17] Stephen Hawking *A Brief History of Time: from Big Bang to Black Holes* (Bantam Press: London), p.193

[18] Epictetus *Discourses* 1.1.7-12: A.A.Long & D.N.Sedley edds., *The Hellenistic Philosophers* (Cambridge University Press: Cambridge 1987), vol.1, p.391 [62K].

indeed, could they act?)[19]. In the last century, however, a disturbing thought has emerged: there seems after all no reason why the cosmos has the laws and balance of forces that it does. It does after all seem 'arbitrary' – an unforced choice - that the fundamental forces (electro-magnetism, weak force, strong force, gravity) have the relations that they do, that elementary particles are as they are, that the universe has expanded at exactly the speed it did, and that there was just enough of an excess of matter over anti-matter that there remains a material universe. Worse still, the precise features of our cosmos seem such that even the slightest variation would have made it impossible for there to be life of anything like our sort at all[20]. The feeblest and silliest response to this has been to say that if things had been different we wouldn't be here to wonder why, and there's an end of the matter – which is like noticing that one has somehow survived a series of lethal lightning strikes and refusing to wonder how this happened, or what other features of the situation were linked to the happy outcome. Others have hoped – in Stoic vein - that it will turn out that somehow or other things *had* to be that way, because of some deeper formula – that only the actual cosmos is a possible one at all (which does not answer the question why there is *any* cosmos, but at least leaves the 'choice' of cosmos comfortingly secure). Theists of many persuasions have seen this 'fine-tuning' as evidence of design: apparently something outside and above all cosmic order 'chooses' to realize just this sort of world, presumably to harvest living, conscious beings from it. But the methodological

[19] For some of the problems with this inchoate assumption see my 'Folly to the Greeks: good reasons to give up reason' in *European Journal for Philosophy of Religion* 4.2012, pp.93-113.

[20] See John D.Barrow, Frank J.Tipler & John A.Wheeler *The Anthropic Cosmological Principle* (Oxford University Press: Oxford 1988; 2nd ed.); Paul Davies *The Goldilocks Enigma: why is the Universe just right for Life?* (Penguin: London 2007).

naturalism that is central to the modern scientific enterprise – a naturalism originally adopted, it should be noted, for theological reasons – makes that theistic inference unpopular, or at least 'unscientific'. Instead mainstream cosmological speculation has moved in an Epicurean direction.

For Epicureans reality is composed of infinitely (countably?) many unbreakable bodies ('atoms') with infinitely many shapes and sizes, and without limits to their motion in either space or time. In that infinite array all possible combinations and life-stories can occur. Some indeed have falsely inferred that all imaginable combinations and life-stories *must* occur[21]: strictly, even if there are infinitely many worlds (uncountably many?) it does not follow that all the infinitely many *possible* worlds are really actual – maybe only every millionth possible world is actual, or every googolth. And not every *imaginable* world is really possible (though what constrains the possibilities we do not know). But it would at least be difficult to insist of any seemingly possible world that it is nowhere ever actual: why wouldn't it be? And Epicureans found evidence that there were such 'actualized possibilities' in our experience of phantoms – shadows cast by alien anatomies. Not all such worlds have anything like human beings in them, nor even living creatures of whatever sort. Granted the conditions it is not odd that we ourselves look out on a world sufficiently accommodating to the development of living creatures just like us as to allow our existence! Or at least no odder than the conditions.

[21] Thus Max Tegmark in 'Parallel Universes' *Scientific American* May 2003, 288.5, pp.41-53: 'in infinite space, even the most unlikely events must take place somewhere'. Tegmark's paper revitalizes the old idea that we each have infinitely many identical or near identical copies, either in a future round of the cosmos (the Stoic notion) or – as Tegmark himself suggests – in other bubble universes immensely far away.

For ancient Epicureans there was a single Space in which the infinitely many 'atoms' fall and swerve and make up larger bodies. In the modern version of the story those Other Universes are not just far away from us within the familiar framework of three-dimensional Space (though there may be other bubbles of 'false vacuum' even within such a framework, so far away that they can never be observed), but may be separate from us in another unfamiliar direction, or else be different episodes in a longer hypercosmic history. Each cosmos begins and possibly ends in a Singularity: the Big Bang or the Big Crunch (though current evidence suggests that *our* cosmos at least is doomed to expand and dissipate forever). In that timeless, spaceless moment the fundamental laws are arbitrarily recast. Or else – in a further twist – they are cast again in every possible way. All possible versions emerge from the Singularity, 'alongside' what we conceive to be the only actual world, but each – from within that version – just as real as ours.

This thought – that all possible versions coexist – has some backing from experiment[22]. Just as there seems no reason why our cosmos should be the only possibility, so also there seems no reason why a given elementary particle should move one way or another. Indeed it seems that we have reason to suppose that, given the chance, it moves all possible ways – which is the currently best explanation for the patterns observed when shining photons, one at a time, onto a screen, through a barrier with two slits. If each photon is left unobserved on its passage through the barrier, it passes through both slits at every possible angle and generates a typical wave pattern on the screen (exactly as if there were many photons passing through). If we watch to see which slit it passes through, it passes through only one and a single dot is visible on the screen. Somehow, our

[22] A lucid and almost persuasive account of this theory can be found in David Deutsch *The Fabric of Reality; towards a theory of everything* (Penguin: London 1998).

observation 'collapses' the possibilities, the wave function. The spooky suggestion was at first that it was only conscious observation that decided the particle's position, as though the bodies with which we share reality were waiting for our observation before deciding where to be. The great physicist Erwin Schrödinger, thinking it absurd to suppose that elementary particles played such games, proposed a thought experiment to demonstrate the absurdity:

> One can even set up quite ridiculous cases. A cat is penned up in a steel chamber, along with the following device (which must be secured against direct interference by the cat): in a Geiger counter there is a tiny bit of radioactive substance, so small, that *perhaps* in the course of the hour one of the atoms decays, but also, with equal probability, perhaps none; if it happens, the counter tube discharges and through a relay releases a hammer which shatters a small flask of hydrocyanic acid. If one has left this entire system to itself for an hour, one would say that the cat still lives *if* meanwhile no atom has decayed. The psi-function of the entire system would express this by having in it the living and dead cat (pardon the expression) mixed or smeared out in equal parts[23].

Schrödinger's opponents had insisted that there was nothing determinate about whether the particle was or was not emitted until a human observation collapsed the wave function. Till then all the possible outcomes existed as 'superpositions of different eigenstates'. Schrödinger pointed out that in his imagined experiment they must thence conclude that the cat was neither alive nor dead until they opened the box to see. This, he thought, was sufficiently silly as to prove that there was some fact of the matter about what the elementary particles were doing, even if we could not ourselves

---

[23] Erwin Schrödinger 'The Present Situation in Quantum Mechanics' (tr. John Trimmer) in *Proceedings of the American Philosophical Society* 124. 1935, pp.323-38 (http://www.tu-harburg.de/rzt/rzt/it/QM/cat.html, accessed 26th April 2012).

detect that fact.[24] Physicists who preferred the 'Copenhagen' interpretation instead concluded that indeed the cat was neither alive nor dead until the box was opened (excusing themselves from wondering whether the *cat* was conscious of its own survival by assuming without adequate argument that cats aren't conscious). This response was made even less acceptable when Eugen Wigner offered a further gloss: the whole experimental set up (cat, box and human experimenter) is established in a further box – the whole laboratory. No-one outside the laboratory can determine before the event whether the cat is alive or dead, *nor whether the experimenter finds the cat alive or dead.* It takes a friend of the experimenter ('Wigner's Friend') to 'collapse the eigenstates'![25] Since human beings – unlike cats – were assumed themselves to be conscious entities capable of observing and so 'collapsing' reality, it seemed absurd to suppose that the experimenter's reality depended wholly on what the Friend observed. 'The being with a consciousness', so Wigner said, 'must have a different role in quantum mechanics than the inanimate measuring device'. This seemed offensive to materialists. The Everett 'Many Worlds' or 'Many Histories' interpretation, once reckoned too absurd to acknowledge, has gradually become the mainstream

[24] Thus John G.Cramer 'The Transactional Interpretation of Quantum Mechanics': *Reviews of Modern Physics* 58.1986, pp.647-688 (http://mist.npl.washington.edu/npl/int_rep/tiqm/TI_toc.html, accessed 23rd April 2012): 'In the period just before the observation is made the SV describes the cat as 50% alive and 50% dead. This description, which may seem plausible enough when applied to a microscopic system (or even to a statistically large ensemble of Schrödinger's cat experiments), appears rather absurd when applied to an individual complex organism like a cat.'

[25] See E.P.Wigner 'Remarks on the Mind-Body Problem':*The Scientist Speculates*, ed. I. J. Good (Heinemann, London 1962), pp.284-302; reprinted in Wigner *Symmetries and Reflections* (Indiana University Press: Bloomington, Indiana 1967) , pp.171-184.

view.[26] There are two equal realities: when the experimenter opens the box one version of him finds the cat alive, and another finds it dead. The observer plays no part in collapsing the wave function – since the wave function has not in fact collapsed, though its elements have 'decohered', and so become mutually inaccessible[27]. Strictly, indeed, there will likely be any number of versions who find the cat is dead – in different postures, different parts of the box, and for different lengths of time. The cat's history has split before the box is opened, as has the experimenter's before Wigner's Friend arrives. The experimenter does not notice that he has been divided: each version is consistent in its opinion. The same argument applies of course to the Friends of Wigner's Friend, who cannot tell – until they check – whether the Friend has found an experimenter with a live cat, or one with a dead cat.

Some theorists – seeking to avoid the multiplication of real worlds and histories by holding to the Copenhagen Intepretation, and to the importance of conscious observers - have concluded that only a Final Observer, at the End of Time, can determine unambiguously what has happened, and that it is *this* Observation that will retrospectively actualize just one particular history. Does it follow that we here-now

---

[26] Hugh Everett '"Relative State" Formulation of Quantum Mechanics': *Reviews of Modern Physics* 29.1957, pp.454-62.

[27] The different versions of photons passing singly through the slits 'interfere' with each other, but go together to make up a coherent macroscopic reality (the wave-pattern on the screen): the different versions of cat, experimenter, friends and friends of friends are divided from each other. Whether they could ever be reunited (and so encounter their alternate versions) is moot: if all imaginably possible worlds are really actual, then presumably there are worlds where this happens (as in several of Diana Wynne-Jones' fantasies: e.g. *Charmed Life* (Macmillan: London 1977), *The Homeward Bounders* (Macmillan: London 1981), *Witch Week* (Macmillan: London 1982) and many others).

are living in a merely 'virtual' possible reality that may not be the one to be actualized at the end of time[28]? Or is that too rough a rejection of the fundamental Cartesian intuition, that I know that I exist here-now, even if I don't exactly 'know' any of the more familiar facts or fancies? But perhaps the Final Observer, timelessly, 'has' actualized the world – and this is indeed the one true history: nothing in fundamental physics after all *requires* that there be no effect from 'the future' on 'the past'. Another version of this 'transactional' interpretation, omitting the Observer, also rests on the equality of all moments in the temporal sequence: what happens to the cat is fixed atemporally because only one outcome is consistent with everything else that happens[29]. Other versions involving an 'objective' – and undetermined – collapse of the wave function suffer from the problem that the collapse apparently must propagate itself at more than the speed of light: suggesting again that there is a level of reality that transcends the material. Yet another theory – echoing the 'Aristotelian' description of Copernicus' heliocentrism offered by Andreas Osiander and later by Cardinal Bellarmine[30]– is that the

[28] Stephen Baxter has played with this idea in *Timelike Infinity* (Collins: London 1992); see also Arthur C.Clarke & Gentry Lee *Rama Revealed* (Gollancz: London 1993).

[29] Cramer op.cit.: 'There is not a "when", not a point in time at which the quantum event is finished. The event is finished when the transaction forms, which happens along a set of world lines which include all of the event listed above, treating none of them as the special conclusion of the event'.

[30]Andreas Osiander 'Introduction' in Nicolaus Copernicus *On the Revolutions of the Heavenly Spheres*, tr.C.G.Wallis (Prometheus Books: New York 1995; 1st published 1939); Robert Bellarmine to Paolo Foscarini, 12th April 1615: 'to say that, assuming the earth moves and the sun stands still, all the appearances are saved better than with eccentrics and epicycles, is to speak well; there is no danger in this, *and it is sufficient for mathematicians*. But to want to affirm that the sun really is fixed in the center of the heavens and only revolves around itself (i.e. turns upon its axis) without traveling from east to west,

whole theoretical apparatus is only a way of predicting actual observations, and that nothing should be inferred about what lies behind the observations: but this, despite having been a dominant mood in earlier decades, is to abandon science![31] Galilean science, at any rate, rests on the *Platonic* assumption that we have intellectual access to the principles of the universe because both the universe and our own intellects have the same transcendent source. In Benedict XVI's words (2009): 'the objective structure of the universe and the intellectual structure of the human being coincide; the subjective reason and the objectified reason in nature are identical. In the end it is "one" reason that links both and invites us to look to a unique creative Intelligence.'[32] The alternative is, in the end, to abandon scientific realism.

The earth really does rotate, and orbit around the sun (or at least that is our present assumption – one that may not be as secure as we suppose). Perhaps the Many Worlds are real as well. At any rate, the preferred version amongst speculative physicists – though it may be that even they do not think much about this in their usual lives - is currently that our cosmos is only one of indefinitely many, each real to its insiders.

According to many-worlds all the possible outcomes of a quantum interaction are realised. The wave function, instead of

---

and that the earth is situated in the third sphere and revolves with great speed around the sun, *is a very dangerous thing'* (http://www.fordham.edu /halsall/mod/1615bellarmine-letter.asp, accessed 24th April 1012: my italics).

[31] See Owen Barfield *Unancestral Voice* (Faber: London 1965).

[32] Benedict XVI to Archbishop Rino Fisichella, on the occasion of the international congress 'From Galileo's Telescope to Evolutionary Cosmology' (30 November – 2 December 2009), http://www.vatican.va/ holy_father/benedict_xvi/messages/pont-messages /2009/documents/hf_ben-xvi_mes_20091126_fisichella-telescopio_en.html (accessed 26th April 2012).

collapsing at the moment of observation, carries on evolving in a deterministic fashion, embracing all possibilities embedded within it. All outcomes exist simultaneously but do not interfere further with each other, each single prior world having split into mutually unobservable but equally real worlds.[33]

In a way that Plotinus could hardly have imagined, all possibilities and levels of reality must be instantiated! In such a universe or multiverse it may seem no surprise that the cosmos and the history we observe is – obviously – one that is compatible with our being here to observe it. We may still be startled that *any* set of laws and forces should be so constructive in their outcome: even if there are infinitely many histories there may still be a question why particular histories are realized. Even if our cosmos (or rather the set of coevolving cosmoi seeded from our Big Bang) is, literally, the only one in all eternity to have the requisite properties – though this seems very unlikely - it may be a source of wonder that it (or they) has happened. But there is a further speculative twist: maybe indeed our cosmos is so superbly fine-tuned precisely because there are agencies involved that have fine-tuned it. Maybe they are themselves the products of an almost infinitely rare chance, whose probability they can 'now' increase. Maybe they arose within a cosmos radically unlike our own: a cosmos, let us suppose, which allowed the very early emergence of life and conscious enterprise, at a time when all its energy was readily at hand[34]. If we cannot legitimately exclude *any* real possibility, then one of the Many Worlds is one united in intelligence and power from very near its beginnings: the Omega

---

[33] http://www.hedweb.com/everett/index.html: Michael Clive Price's Everett FAQ, Q2 (accessed 22nd April 2012).

[34] Some of these speculations have been explored by Stephen Baxter, for example in *Exultant: Destiny's Children Book Two* (Gollancz: London 2004) and *The Time Ships* (Collins: London 1995).

World, rather than the Omega Point of Chardin's – and Olaf Stapledon's - imaginings[35]! However They arose in their beginnings, they can be supposed to have access to sufficient power, skill, information to engineer new cosmoi, whether through the Singularity (which is, for us, the moment when all laws and extrapolations fail) or through the creation of 'black holes' (which are, in some current theories, the gateways to new cosmoi, potentially with different laws and balances of power)[36]. Maybe they are our own successors, bending back in time to create themselves and us! But if that is to be thought possible it seems more likely that we have been forestalled – and not necessarily by intelligences that much resemble us: our sort of intelligence, as far as we know, has evolved only once in terrestrial history, whereas - for example - eusocial insects are a far commoner form, and more to be expected, on merely naturalistic grounds, Out There[37]! But more of the observable cosmos than we think may turn out to be the effect of living purposes of some sort, and Plotinus was right to insist that it was Soul that made all worlds[38]. He may even have been right to suggest that the different cycles of world history (for he was ready to consider, with the Stoics and with some modern physicists, that the number of possible entities was finite, and their combinations must eventually be exhausted) could be subtly different[39]: each soul was allocated, perhaps, a different role to play in

[35] See my 'Olaf Stapledon (1886-1950)': Ellis op.cit., pp.355-70.

[36] James N. Gardner *The Intelligent universe : AI, ET, and the emerging mind of the cosmos* (New Page Books: Franklin Lakes, N.J. 2007).

[37] See my 'God, Reason and Extraterrestrials' in *God, Mind and Knowledge*, ed., Andrew Moore (Ashgate: London, forthcoming).

[38] *Ennead* V.1 [10]. 2.

[39] Plotinus *Ennead* V.7 [18].1; see also *Ennead* III.7 [45].11. See Richard Sorabji *Time, Creation and the Continuum: theories in antiquity and the early Middle Ages* (Duckworth: London 1983), p.18.

the cosmic theatre next time round, depending on its previous success![40] And how many more performances before we get it right? The idea that Soul in general, and our souls, have their origin elsewhere, outside the material frame of the many cosmoi, is not one easily admitted by modern cosmologists wedded to a methodological materialism – but in the absence of any adequate theory how material motions could generate conscious experience it has to remain a serious possibility.[41]

And what is the relevance of this speculative cosmology to the immediate practicalities of our life here and now? Whether the Stoics were right to think that there is only one, finite cosmos, and that it could not be otherwise, or the Epicureans right to think that there were infinitely many, it seems that we have no choices. Either all that possibly could happen, does, or else what doesn't happen, can't: the two claims are logically equivalent, though the former sounds less restrictive! Either way we here-now are doing all and only what we can: even if Epicureans and modern physicists are right that there are other versions of ourselves doing and observing other things, whether in Everett's Many Worlds or in immensely distant bubble universes, the very fact that 'they' are doing that means that 'we' can't be – except in the useless sense, available also to Stoics, that creatures very much like us do other things than we do. Our being –

---

[40] See *Ennead* III.2 [47].17, 45-53.

[41] The main alternative accounts of 'mind-body' interaction are eliminative materialism (according to which our conscious experience is a fiction) and naturalistic panpsychism (according to which all material elements have psychological properties that somehow add up, in multicellular creatures, to experience). Neither of these accounts strikes me as more plausible than Platonism: see my *From Athens to Jerusalem* (Clarendon Press: Oxford 1984), pp.121-57. Both have very strange ethical implications, largely ignored by theorists! But that is another story.

the being of all the different versions of ourselves - is fixed and cannot be any different. Platonists can plausibly disagree: for them, the choice of lives and worlds occurs outside the frame, and not all possibilities are actual[42]. We choose or have chosen this world and history here: we are in a way in the place of the Final Observer, actualizing one history from all the possibilities[43]. Or at least this is a possibility unknown to the Stoic – or Epicurean – fatalist. Platonism better accommodates the assumptions implicit in scientific speculation: that there is a discoverable order to the world, that we can be guided to its discovery by seeking mathematical beauty, and that we ought to try. For Epicureans, strictly, there is no order on which we could reasonably count; for Stoics – and especially for the atheistical, modern sort - there is no principle outside or before the world's reality which would ever serve to explain why *this* world does exist, nor why we should expect it to continue.

But though – in a way – we *might* be in the place of the Final Observer, it is perhaps more likely, or at least more seemly, to suggest that the Final Observer might be very unlike us, whether It collapses all the superposited histories into one coherent strand or else stands at the end of them all, look backing at all the confluent pasts that lead to the Singularity, the Conflagration or the Omega Point – as though the infinitely many particles, each taking all its possible routes, form at last the complete wave pattern of the cosmos

---

[42] See Plotinus *Ennead* III.1 [3].8-9.

[43] One further really weird suggestion – perhaps intended as a reduction of theories that emphasise the effects of observation - is that our present day observation of 'dark matter' may have shortened the life of the cosmos, by collapsing the possibilities: Leonard M.Krauss & James Dent 'Late Time Behavior of False Vacuum Decay: Possible Implications for Cosmology and Metastable Inflating States' in *Physical Review Letters* 100.2008, pp.171301-4 (DOI: 10.1103/PhysRevLett.100.171301).

on the Observer's screen. Maybe we are each accompanied by a shadow counterpart (for whom, of course, *we* are the shadow counterpart) who has done different things, for better or worse, with our opportunities. Or maybe the wave function has 'already' been collapsed by the Final Observer, and we are in truth the only actual line. Or else we can use a different myth, to very much the same effect: our cosmos has been seeded – perhaps by Engineers at the imagined 'end of time' – with a view to producing us – and maybe producing the Engineers: a speculation that some theorists seem to suppose would be a satisfactory explanation (the Engineers exist because they engineered, from the End of Time, the cosmos that produced them in its 'earlier' phase)[44]. But the one thing that in either case is standing alongside us is, precisely, the Final Observer or the Final Engineer. Something has selected us from all the possibilities as Its companions in the timeless moment. Which is what theists had already said:

From all eternity [God] chose us from among an infinite number of possible beings. He chose us, not those other possible beings, and so they did not exist. And among all these others he also chose you, individually. He chose you from an infinity of possible beings who could have existed but whom he did not create. You were the one chosen from an infinite number of possibilities, and the very fact that you exist is the greatest proof of god's preference for you. Each of us is irreplaceable. We are all unique

---

[44] See Davies op.cit. p.283, after John A.Wheeler 'World as a system self-synthesized by quantum networking': *IBM Journal of Research and Development* 32.1988, pp.4-15. Wheeler (ibid., p.14) orates as follows: 'Life and mind: For how much can they be conceived to count in the scheme of existence? Nothing, say the billions of light years of space that lie around us. Everything, say the billions of years of time that lie ahead of us.'

collectors' pieces, because god is an artist who never repeats or reproduces himself.[45]

On the one account (the currently mainstream cosmological account) all possible versions of myself and all possible versions of human history and all possible versions even of an expanding cosmos are just as real as the ones that seem, parochially, 'actual'. Correspondingly, all possible *futures* (from our point of view) are also real, and 'we' shall be enduring them all, even though each version of ourselves experiences only one. Whatever possibility is realized in our singular experience we shall know – if we believe this argument – that every other possibility has been realized as well. There is no privileged place or moment, scale or version, such that it alone is 'real' or 'central'. Whatever happens can be no surprise, and require no further explanation (though the fundamental mystery, of existence, still remains). Whatever happens will turn out to be following the forms, even if not in the way that we here-now expect.

Alternatively – and following the strangely attractive speculation that only this actual world has been 'chosen' from beyond its bounds, by our own spiritual selves, or by the Final Engineer, or by an Unknown God – the reasons for this actual world cannot be found within the world. 'According to the Aristotelian paradigm, physical reality is fundamental and mathematical language is merely a useful approximation. According to the Platonic paradigm, the mathematical structure is the true reality and observers perceive it imperfectly.'[46] Things don't *have* to be this way – and we may wonder

[45] Ernesto Cardenal *Love*, tr. Dinah Livingstone (Paraclete Press: Brewster, Mass. 2006), p.25.

[46] Tegmark op.cit., p.49. The 'Aristotelian' mode described is not entirely true to Aristotle (for whom a non-material Unmoved *Nous* was the ultimate explanation), and the 'Platonic' omits what mattered most to Plato and his disciples: namely, the Good. Mathematical Reality is not, for Plato, ultimate.

why they are, and wonder how we or our successors or creators might do otherwise. That way, we might say, lies Leibniz!

Synthesis

Things don't have to be this way – and perhaps they aren't.

I have spoken of two Singularities: the cosmic, and the social. The cosmic Singularity, the Big Bang and the – possible - Big Crunch, is that moment when all laws fail, all separate entities are dissolved in the primordial Atum, the world-mound of Egyptian story, or in the Emptiness that stood behind and around the world, symbolized as a snake.

> This earth will return to the primeval water (Nun), to endless (flood) as in its first state. I [that is Atum] shall remain with Osiris after I have transformed myself into another snake [Apopis] which men do not know and the gods do not see.[47]

The Egyptian titles might mislead the literal-minded – but so do the much more vulgar titles that 20th century cosmologists invented! 'The Big Bang' was not an explosion, and 'the Big Crunch' (if it happens) will not be a train wreck: rather the events signal the beginning (or the end) of spatio-temporal distinctions. 'Then' there was only a 'false

---

One oddity in Davies' otherwise clear and well-informed account of cosmological speculation is his suggestion that 'abandoning Platonism would make room for teleology' (op.cit., p.266), as though Plato thought that mathematical objects, and the mathematically expressed 'laws of nature' were self-explanatory, or that the laws *we have identified* are bound to be permanent. Davies also appears to share the odd idea that 'teleology' is a form of backward causation!

[47] *Book of the Dead* ch.175, cited by Eric Hornung *Conceptions of God in Ancient Egypt*, tr. John Baines (Cornell University Press Ithaca NY 1982, p.163).

vacuum' (misleadingly so called) by contrast with the 'true' vacuum we inhabit, where the four fundamental forces – electromagnetism, gravity, weak and strong nuclear forces – are distinct (though more recently it has been suspected that ours is only another 'false' – and unstable - vacuum). Nothing can be extrapolated back or forward through that Moment, though this has not prevented speculative cosmologists (as above) from devising literally metaphysical tales about what goes on before or after or around. The social Singularity, when Moore's Law works its final magic, is the moment when our artefacts so far exceed our grasp as to make their aims and methods utterly inscrutable to us, though this has not prevented speculative futurologists from wondering how to join or to resist them. The social Singularity differs from all other social transformations: hopefully, we shall find that 'we shall all be changed, in a moment, in the twinkling of an eye, at the last trumpet; for the trumpet will sound, and the dead will be raised imperishable, and we shall be changed'[48].

But maybe that will not work out as optimistic futurologists suppose. Back in Babylon it was accepted that human beings had been created as convenient labourers – and their creators often tired of them. In the Abrahamic tradition it was believed instead that the Creator had appointed Adam as His image and in His likeness, and that every individual human was therefore owed the respect, almost the worship, that in other traditions was owed only to kings, priests and heroes. In paying that respect we might also hope to recover the likeness which Adam lost: to be 'holy' (which is to say, compassionate) as God is holy[49]. The Pauline prophecy, and the

---

[48] 1 *Corinthians* 15:50-52.

[49] See Eliezer Berkovits *Man and God: studies in Biblical Theology* (Wayne State University Press: Detroit 1969) on *qadosh*; William Schweiker, Michael A.Johnson & Kevin Jung edds., *Humanity Before God: contemporary faces of Jewish, Christian and Islamic Ethics* (Fortress Press: Minneapolis 2006).

Christian tradition about 'theosis', was that we would become as gods: that, after all was why God became man, so that human beings could become God.[50] This hope, for the futurologists, is to be vindicated by technology, as we are caught up into the Computer or mated with our non-biological offspring. On Kurzweil's guess or prophecy 'the entire universe will become saturated with our intelligence'[51]. But both cosmological and sociological speculation seems instead to point towards a time when we shall have returned to Babylon, or be cast down still further. Our cosmic future is likely to be determined by vast powers beyond our reach, and our immediate future by computerized intelligence. Judgment Day may be coming[52]. Even if those powers are – as the more optimistic futurologists have supposed – our 'children' and successors, inheritors of the dream, we have no idea what form that dream will take in them. The more familiar sorts of human being – ones who won't or can't be copied or absorbed into the Computers - will probably survive as servitors or pets or vermin. This may also offer an explanation of the Fermi Paradox or Puzzle: if intelligent life is as common in the universe as theory suggests, why has it not come visiting[53]? But perhaps the

[50] Athanasius *On the Incarnation* ch.54.3; see Norman Russell *The Doctrine of Deification in the Greek Patristic Tradition* (Oxford University Press: Oxford 2006; 2nd ed.).

[51] Kurzweil op.cit., p.29; see also p.361, citing his *The Age of Spiritual Machines* (Viking Press: New York 1998), pp.258-60: 'intelligence will ultimately prove more powerful than ... big impersonal forces', and it will be up to 'us' or our successors to decide how the universe will end.

[52] As the more pessimistic SF writers have suggested: see, for example, *The Terminator* (directed by James Cameron, 1984), *Terminator 2: Judgment Day* (directed by James Cameron, 1993).

[53] See Stephen Webb *If the Universe is Teeming with Aliens, Where is Everybody? Fifty Solutions to the Fermi Paradox and the Problem of Extraterrestrial Life* (Copernicus Books: New York 2002).

answer is a simple one: any intelligences smart and powerful enough to travel or transmit themselves and their ideas across galactic space will have no interest in us – unless perhaps as relics, whether obsolete or engaging.

That last judgement of course may tell us more about the habits and ideas of certain *human beings* than any imagined superbeings. In the very act of insisting that those beings will be utterly unlike us, the pessimists suggest that they will be like the most indifferent and short-sighted of human adventurers, as though indifference and discourtesy were obvious markers of high intelligence. What humanists, in the Hellenic as well as the Abrahamic tradition, have previously supposed is that human beings are significantly different from the non-human precisely in that we do take an interest in all other creatures, and are not bound by species-specific feelings. That interest may often have been patronizing. It may even have been used and promoted to give us ways of manipulating others: the advantage of our understanding other creatures may often have been that we could avoid their attack, hunt them down, domesticate and exploit them. But that manipulative use has often also been decried: even if shepherds are exploiting sheep, they may also love and give their lives for them, and there have always been firm limits on how much a decent shepherd can exploit his flock.

> Prophesy, man, against the shepherds of Israel: prophesy and say to them, You shepherds, these are the words of the Lord God: How I hate the shepherds of Israel who care only for themselves! Should not the shepherd care for the sheep? You consume the milk, wear the wool, and slaughter the fat beasts but you don't feed the sheep. You have not encouraged the weary, tended the sick, bandaged the hurt, recovered the straggler, or searched for the lost; and even the strong you have driven with ruthless severity. ... I will dismiss these shepherds: they shall care only for

themselves no longer; I will rescue my sheep from their jaws, and they shall feed on them no longer[54].

It is not impossible that our successors or supplanters will behave a little better than we do. To suggest that they are likelier to behave like Winthrop's colonists – vowing to do justice and love mercy while simultaneously excusing themselves for obvious injustice and neglect – is simply to project our own confusions and desires on beings which, by hypothesis, have other motives and far better understandings. We have no good ground ourselves for despising other creatures for not being 'intellectual' enough, when they so obviously surpass us in so many other ways. As Aristotle said, there is something wonderful and beautiful in even the smallest, commonest and apparently 'base' of living creatures[55]. The superbeings we are imagining may reasonably think the same of us: there will be things that we can do which they cannot, however strange their powers. At the least we should hope that they have learnt two lessons: not to despise those that in some ways they surpass, lest they themselves be despised by even greater powers, and not to despise the achievements of the past, lest their successors do so too.[56]

Is there a natural route to the realization of that hope? We can fairly safely assume that all living creatures seek to live, and also to spread

---

[54] *Ezekiel* 34.1ff. Obviously, in its prophetic context this is a rebuke specifically to the rulers of Israel, who had broken their covenant to care for the weak and poor in their community. But the metaphor makes no sense unless literal shepherds were expected to care for sheep.

[55] Aristotle *De Partibus Animalium* 1.645a15f.

[56] See John C.Wright *The Golden Age: a romance of the far future* (Tor: New York 2002), *The Phoenix Exultant* (Tor: New York 2003), *The Golden Transcendence, or The Last of the Masquerade* (Tor: New York 2003).

their life. Some may fall into the trap of remorseless growth, *pleonexia* – the philosophy of cancer[57]. Those who survive will have discovered cooperation. Our own bodies are evidence of this: founded, like all multicellular eukaryotes, on the willing cooperation both of their own cells, and of our bacterial partners[58]. Our very cells are fuelled by mitochondrial bacteria (with their own DNA), and our digestion depends on other bacterial forms. We cannot survive as individuals without the support of a biosphere, or without the support of our close kindred and our cousins. The same will be true even of the superbeings, whether we are thinking of computer intelligences that come to life in the World Wide Web or of beings from the End of Time, who must rely on a network of fuel and communication beyond our power to conceive, in 'a universe growing without limit in richness and complexity, a universe of life surviving forever and making itself known to its neighbors across unimaginable gulfs of space and time'[59].

One further feature of intelligence is that it *imagines* possibilities in order to learn how to deal with them more safely if they are ever realized – and also to enjoy them. Sometimes we imagine simpler possibilities than we are likely to encounter, whether as training exercises or to discover the essential lessons more clearly than we can in 'real life'. The same, we can fairly safely say, will be true for our superbeings. They will entertain and train themselves, engage with simple fantasies and simplified histories in order to discover in

[57] Edward Abbey *Desert Solitaire: a season in the wilderness* (Touchstone: New York 1968), p.127: 'Growth for the sake of growth is a cancerous madness'.

[58] See Lynn Margulis & Dorion Sagan *Microcosmos: four billion years of microbial evolution* (Berkeley: University of California Press, 1997; 2nd edition).

[59] Freeman J.Dyson 'Time without End: Physics and Biology in an Open Universe' (1979) in *Selected Papers of Freeman Dyson* (American Mathematical Society: Providence, Rhode Island 1996), pp.529-42: p.541

themselves the virtues they may need to face the long night coming, or whatever stranger creatures cosmic evolution in all its variants has thrown up. They will create what we call 'virtual realities': cruder and simpler than their own real lives together, but adequately scripted for those who dip down into them, and for the creatures they create to populate the play.

Does this sound familiar?

> Even before this coming to be we were there, men who were different, and some of us even gods, pure souls and intellect united with the whole of reality; we were parts of the intelligible, not marked off or cut off but belonging to the whole; and we are not cut off even now.[60]

This thought has at least two echoes in current cosmological and futurological speculation. Futurologists, noticing the growth of virtual reality for entertainment and research, have also noticed that there could easily come a time when almost all experiences, say, of 21st century European life will in fact be simulations, entered out of ennui, adventurous spirit or sociological observation. It follows that we ourselves – you and I united in the reading of this paragraph – are far more likely to be experiencing a simulation![61] In Dainton's words:

> Although it seems to you that you are a normal human being living at the start of the 21st century, the subjects of all the many artificially produced type-21 streams have very similar experiences and beliefs. These subjects are all mistaken, and so

[60] Plotinus *Enneads* VI.4 [22].14, 18ff: *The Enneads*, tr.A.H.Armstrong (London: Loeb Classical Library, Heinemann 1966-88), vol.6, p.317. All quotations from Plotinus are drawn from Armstrong's translation.

[61] Nick Bostrom 'Are You Living in a Computer Simulation?' in *Philosophical Quarterly* 53.2003, pp.243-255 (http://www.simulation-argument.com/simulation.pdf, accessed 18th April 2010); Barry Dainton 'On Singularities and Simulations' in *Journal of Consciousness Studies* **19**. 2012, pp.42–85.

might you be, for it is more likely than not that you *are* one of these subjects[62].

This conclusion is reinforced if we look beyond the immediate social Singularity to the working of whatever intelligences stand at the End of Time, and especially if we take account of the Many Worlds Interpretation. Granted that this scenario is *possible* (and there seems no reason to doubt it) it would be actualized in indefinitely many of the variant histories, and at indefinitely many periods within each history. Almost certainly, we are dreaming – and whether there ever was a 'real' original 21st century – in multiple original versions - is moot (and maybe unimportant)[63]! The fact that the dream is

---

[62] Dainton op.cit., p.57.

[63] That the real world is very unlike our experience has seemed to some to make the simulation argument self-defeating: if in fact there are no such technical achievements as are used to suggest that we might soon develop virtual realities then we do not in fact have reason – though we thought we did – to expect that we are living in such simulations – though in actual fact we are. The evidence from which we draw what is – by hypothesis - the correct conclusion can only have been inserted into the dream as a sort of hint to us, but has no real evidential authority. As Democritus agreed, we are drawing our evidence that the senses deceive us from what our senses tell us (DK68B11)! I am not persuaded that this subverts the argument. Dainton op.cit., pp.67-71 argues that – in order not to make the argument self-defeating - we are entitled to believe that the simulation is not *too* different from the real world: on this too I am not wholly persuaded. One further problem with the conception, after all, is that even the experience of the superbeings will be subject to the same uneasy doubt, and that no-one will *ever* know that s/he is not dreaming, unless their experience is indeed very different from ours, and more certainly united with reality. See my 'Waking-Up: a neglected model for the afterlife': *Inquiry* 26.1983, pp.209-30; and 'A Plotinian Account of Intellect': *American Catholic Philosophical Quarterly* 71.1997, pp.421-32, after Plotinus *Ennead* V.5 [32].1.

sometimes very frightening is no argument against its being created – nor even against our having volunteered to dream it (though we may also have been kidnapped or imprisoned for some fault – or created merely in the simulation as plausible stock characters). Maybe the earth is *not* revolving around the sun! The hypothesis is also an unexpected answer to the Fermi Paradox: if it is very likely that intelligent beings have evolved and prospered elsewhere why do we see no sign of these extraterrestrials here-now? The answer is that all sign of them has been deliberately excluded from this dream – both to encourage the dreamers to attend to their own affairs, and to provide one of those tantalizing hints (of covert contradiction) that may alert a few to our real situation! Almost the only feature of our experience that counts against the hypothesis is that our experience is sometimes *boring*! Would a competent creator of virtual realities not arrange for the experience at least to be *interesting*, at least in the perspective of its clients? But perhaps it is up to us to *make* it interesting – or be summarily closed down.[64]

The second echo is the cosmological. One other route to the Many Worlds Interpretation is through considering the cosmos as the enactment of a sort of computer program – a notion that is indeed implicit in the very idea of a working, transformative formula. The simplest program to produce our cosmos would be the most generous.

In general, computing all evolutions of all universes is much cheaper in terms of information requirements than computing just one particular, arbitrarily chosen evolution. Why? Because the Great Programmer's algorithm that systematically enumerates and runs all universes (with all imaginable types of physical laws, wave functions, noise etc.) is *very* short (although it takes time).

[64] See Kurzweil op.cit., pp.404-5.

On the other hand, computing just one particular universe's evolution (with, say, one particular instance of noise), without computing the others, tends to be very expensive, because almost all individual universes are incompressible, as has been shown above. More is less![65]

Imagine that the programmer is faced by the initial blank that our predecessors called 'the Unlimited': there are indefinitely many variables to define to get things going. The simplest solution – indeed almost the only rational solution – is to say that each variable be assigned all possible values, in all possible combinations. How else, after all, should the programmer discover what the effects would be – except by running exactly that program if only 'in his mind'[66]? The only way, even for a Creator who knows all that is to be known, to

---

[65] Juergen Schmidhuber 'A Computer Scientist's View of Life, the Universe, and Everything': In C. Freksa, ed., *Foundations of Computer Science: Potential - Theory – Cognition: Lecture Notes in Computer Science* (Springer: 1997), pp.201-208 (retrieved from http://www.idsia.ch/~juergen/everything/, 23rd April 2012). There are other features of Schnidhuber's speculation (notably the difficulties it raises for inductive inference, and for his apparent, self-refuting, belief that there is only matter in motion, without even subjective meaning) that deserve longer consideration. See also S.Wolfram *A New Kind of Science* (WolframMedia Inc.: Champaign, IL 2002); Seth Lloyd *Programming the Universe:a quantum computer scientist takes on the cosmos* (Cape: London 2006).

[66] See Plotinus *Ennead* V.8 [31].7, dismissing the idea that the world can have been created: to do so, the Creator must *already* have the world complete 'in His mind'. In the vocabulary of the Christian Church, the Logos is begotten (and of one substance with the Father), and not made (on which see G.L.Prestige *God in Patristic Thought* (SPCK: London 1952), p.151), and what has been made was not put together by hands or other tools, but simply by and through that Logos. But this is yet another story.

know what some programs do is actually to run the programs[67]. So the Creator runs that simple program, and it generates all really possible worlds, with exactly the effect we notice: many such worlds evaporate or expand too slowly or too quickly to accomplish anything distinctive; many stagnate or dissolve in mutual hostility. Whether there are any conscious observers in these worlds depends on factors that we don't understand – not knowing even how or whether material connections somehow 'generate' the conscious mind or merely invite it in, we can't tell which worlds, from their mere material nature, will have minds in them, nor which worlds – if minds in fact come into the world from somewhere completely other – will be colonized. This world at any rate – or the set of worlds that share at least our beginnings – is being lived from within.

Is this story simply a way of speaking? Things are *as if* they were programmed into being, and it is *as if* we are living in a virtual drama. Maybe so – but this merely operationalist account of scientific theory itself suggests that we are dreaming, and can never expect to grasp the *reality* behind our experience. The paradox is that the current picture of that unseen reality is drawing so heavily on the older myth, and issuing in the older moral. This life, this world, is a dream and a delusion, but one that hints to us of some superior power and beauty.

The realities we see are like shadows of all that is God. The reality we see is as unreal compared to the reality in God as a coloured

---

[67] See Kurzweil op.cit., p.93: 'Wolfram makes the valid point that certain (indeed most) computational processes are not predictable. In other words, we cannot predict future states without running the entire process.' The same point applies to the evolutionary history of life here on Earth: it is more difficult to distinguish Design and Darwin than most neo-Darwinian theorists acknowledge!

photograph compared to what it represents. ... This whole world is made of shadows, shadows on the wall of a cave, as Plato said.[68]

The speculative cosmologists are drawing on an older story, and – in part – are offering an older moral. But there is one way at least in which the morals differ. If there is ever to be a fully cosmic intelligence owing anything to human history then the moral is that we should keep the research grants coming![69] The older moral was that, to be acceptable to God, we should do justice and love mercy, as John Winthrop said. The technophile's enthusiasm may rest on a worthy basis: on a real delight in beauty, and a conviction that we can somehow come to share – so to call it – in 'the mind of God'. But that Mind, in the older synthesis, was the 'dance of immortal love'[70], and the 'intelligence' that was to be our guide was better known as love. In drawing on the resources of past philosophy that, perhaps, should be what we chiefly learn, and teach.

Intellect ... has one power for thinking, by which it looks at the things in itself, and one by which it looks at what transcends it by a direct awareness and reception, by which also before it saw only, and by seeing acquired intellect and is one. And that first one is the contemplation of Intellect in its right mind, and the other is Intellect in love, when it goes out of its mind 'drunk with the nectar'; then it falls in love, simplified into happiness by

[68] Cardenal op.cit., pp.73, 91.

[69] See, for example, Frank J.Tipler *The Physics of Immortality: Modern Cosmology, God and the Resurrection of the Dead* (Doubleday: New York 1994). Kurzweil op.cit., p405 similarly proposes that the reason for the simulations is mainly to create 'new knowledge', and the best way to avoid being closed down is to continue studying physics (in what is, by hypothesis, a simplified model of the unseen reality).

[70] Porphyry *Life of Plotinus* 23.36f, after 22.54ff.

having its fill, and it is better for it to be drunk with a drunkenness like this than to be more respectably sober[71].

To wake up from the dream – or at least to realize that we are dreaming – is to be animated by our recognition of what's really real and beautiful. The stories that we tell about that waking, and about the real world we have – deliberately? – forgotten cannot be verified by any experiment here-now. They can only be vindicated (or not) by whether or not we can actually live by them. In making the attempt we can take inspiration, intellectual and moral, from the work of past philosophers, and especially from Platonists.

Coda

Self-conscious moderns often suggest that life and consciousness are at best peripheral: an accidental froth within the larger, unmeaning and insensate world. They may even admit that, on those terms, there is little reason to expect that we – a particular hominid species on a ball of rock – could have the equipment to discover any truth about that world. 'The Universe is not only queerer than we suppose, but queerer than we *can* suppose'[72]. We cannot prove otherwise, even if our faith in reason is partly vindicated – so we think – by the coherence of our speculations and the power of our technology. That faith is at least a little easier if we can also believe that reality is, in some way, suited to us.

That very many, or infinitely many, worlds are actual is really the death of explanation: whatever happens is only what is bound to happen somewhere, and it might as well be here. It is also the death

---

[71] *Enneads* VI.7 [38].35

[72] J.B.S.Haldane *Possible Worlds and Other Essays* (Heinemann: London 1927), p.286.

of purpose: whatever we propose as a possible course of action will be what happens, whether in one of the many real futures or in some far off bubble universe. A similar conclusion follows, as their critics argued, from the strictly Stoic notion, that there is only one real world and history, which must repeat itself in infinite time – and maybe infinite space as well. Stoic philosophers hoped that it could be shown that just this actual world was the only *possible* world as well, or the only one that embodied an eternal, necessary good. And though they sought to reject the fatalistic moral – that it won't matter what we do or try to do – it is hard to see why we should try to avoid error or seek out the truth. Whatever it is we end up doing or believing is what the Universe requires of us, and there is no escape.

The Platonic analysis of our situation seeks to distinguish the phenomenal worlds that sentient creatures severally inhabit from the physical world of bodies arrayed in space and changing over time. That physical world in turn is to be explained by reference to a mathematical system, intuited or remembered by creatures equipped to do so: those 'laws of nature' are never perfectly obeyed, those forms are never perfectly embodied. Nor are they the ultimate explanation: mathematicians, so Plato remarked, forget to explain where their firm concepts come from, or why one system rather than another – equally coherent – system is the model for the physical universe. The laws of nature don't explain why anything exists, nor why they are *these* laws. His hope instead was that there was an explanation, in a transcendent Good, the One. Things as they are – and also our own reason – are modelled on the forms implicit in an eternal intellect: ways of being beautiful. That criterion, of beauty, is invoked in judging scientific theories, even though we must also recognize that our private notions of beauty may not be the ones that eventually we learn to love, and that we cannot rule out the unexpected and bizarre from our appreciation of reality. The Universe is *not* queerer than we can imagine – or at least we had better not imagine that it is – but it may be queerer than we first suppose!

Modern speculations weirdly reproduce the debates and stories of earlier, 'unscientific' generations. And the very weirdest speculation – that we are inmates of a virtual reality devised by the Cosmic Engineers of the End of Days – is at once a sort of resolution of our current cosmological problems, and an inspiration to return to a more strictly Platonic outlook. 'Whether it's reality or a dream, doing what's right is what matters. If it's reality, then for the sake of reality; if it's a dream, then for the purpose of winning friends for when we awaken'[73]. Our best recourse is to do justice, to love mercy, and to remember that we owe our life and reason to powers beyond our control and present understanding. We had better hope that our successors and perhaps creators have internalized that message too.

[73] Calderón de la Barca *Life's A Dream* (University Press of Colorado: Boulder, Colorado 2004; 1st published as *La vida es sueño* in 1635), p.137f.

The Dublin Centre
for the Study of the Platonic Tradition
www.tcd.ie/Classics/cspt

In 2006, The Dublin Centre for the Study of the Platonic Tradition inaugurated an ongoing series of public lectures on the general theme of 'Platonism and the World Crisis' (see Introduction). The purpose here was to invite eminent figures from Irish intellectual and cultural life to deliver a public lecture on a topic that comes under the aegis of the series theme. These lectures are now being published in pamphlet form as a permanent record of these evenings. This series was conceived to become the public face of the Centre, the visible aspect of our existence, so to speak; but what of the Centre itself as a scholarly institution, its main *raison d'etre?* Who are we and what do we do?

General Introduction

The Centre, founded in 1997, is designed to coordinate and direct activities in the area of the history of Platonism (including Christian, Jewish and Islamic Platonism) in the Greater Dublin area, bringing together scholars working at Trinity College, Dublin, the National University of Ireland-Dublin, and the National University of Ireland-Maynooth, together with All Hallows College, Drumcondra.

Its activities include:
- the organising of seminars, colloquia and lectures by visiting scholars
- the supervision of graduate students
- the publication of texts and monographs.

In cooperation with the various constituent departments, the Centre offers degrees in Platonic Studies from Master's through to Doctoral levels.

The Centre Library and Reading Room

On October 21, 2004, there took place the formal opening by the Provost, Prof John Hegarty, of the Library and Reading Room of the Centre. This is the culmination of some years of planning, and resulted from the acceptance by Trinity College of the offer by the Director, Professor John Dillon to offer his library of books of Greek philosophy to the College on condition that premises would be made available to house it. Space was found in the lower level of the 1937 Reading Room in Front Square, and so the Centre now at last has a physical base, and a useful research tool in the form of a collection of about 2500 books on the history of Platonism, together with all of the basic primary texts. This marks the Centre collection as the largest concentration of materials relating to Platonism in the country. Students also have. of course, access to the holdings of the Main Library, which are considerable.

The Stephen MacKenna Lecture Series

Apart from the present series, the Centre hosts a more academic lecture series, named in honour of the great Irish translator of Plotinus, Stephen MacKenna, designed to honour a succession of the most distinguished scholars in the area of Neoplatonism. As of 2010, this has passed into its tenth year, having on May 19 hosted Prof Christopher Gill. Previous MacKenna lecturers include Prof Werner Beierwaltes (1999), Prof John M Rist (2001), Prof Carlos Steel of the University of Leuven (2002), Prof Dominic O'Meara (2005), Professor Eyjolfur Emilsson of Oslo (2006), and Prof Christopher Rowe (2009).

The International Plato Society

The Centre had the honour of holding the Presidency of the International Plato Society, a position that is held for three years, culminating in a major conference, which was held in Trinity College in July 2007.

The Prometheus Trust Catalogue

Platonic Texts and Translations Series

The Thomas Taylor Series

1 Proclus' Elements of Theology

Proclus' Elements of Theology - 211 propositions which frame the metaphysics of the Late Athenian Academy. 978-1-898910-00-8

2 Select Works of Porphyry

Abstinence from Animal Food; Auxiliaries to the Perception of Intelligibles; Concerning Homer's Cave of the Nymphs; Taylor on the Wanderings of Ulysses. 978-1-898910-01-5

3 Collected Writings of Plotinus

Twenty-seven treatises being all the writings of Plotinus translated by Taylor. 978-1-898910-02-2

4 Writings on the Gods & the World

Sallust On the Gods & the World; Sentences of Demophilus; Ocellus on the Nature of the Universe; Taurus and Proclus on the Eternity of the World; Maternus on the Thema Mundi; The Emperor Julian's Orations to the Mother of Gods and to the Sovereign Sun; Synesius on Providence; Taylor's essays on the Mythology and the Theology of the Greeks. 978-1-898910-03-9

5 Hymns and Initiations

The Hymns of Orpheus together with all the published hymns translated or written by Taylor; Taylor's 1824 essay on Orpheus (together with the 1787 version). 978-1-898910-04-6

6 Dissertations of Maximus Tyrius

Forty-one treatises from the middle Platonist, and an essay from Taylor, The Triumph of the Wise Man over Fortune. 978-1-898910-05-3

7 Oracles and Mysteries

A Collection of Chaldean Oracles; Essays on the Eleusinian and Bacchic Mysteries; The History of the Restoration of the Platonic Theology; On the Immortality of the Soul. 978-1-898910-06-0

8 The Theology of Plato

The six books of Proclus on the Theology of Plato; to which is added a further book (by Taylor), replacing the original seventh book by Proclus, now lost. Extensive introduction and notes are also added. 978-1-898910-07-7

9 Works of Plato I

Taylor's General Introduction, Life of Plato, First Alcibiades (with much of Proclus' Commentary), Republic (with a section of Proclus' Commentary). 978-1-898910-08-4

10 Works of Plato II

Laws, Epinomis, Timæus (with notes from Proclus' Commentary), Critias. 978-1-898910-09-1

11 Works of Plato III

Parmenides (with a large part of Proclus' Commentary), Sophista, Phædrus (with notes from Hermias' Commentary), Greater Hippias, Banquet. 978-1-898910-10-7

12 Works of Plato IV

Theætetus, Politicus, Minos, Apology of Socrates, Crito, Phædo (with notes from the Commentaries of Damascius and Olympiodorus), Gorgias (with notes from the Commentary of Olympiodorus), Philebus (with notes from the Commentary of Olympiodorus), Second Alcibiades. 978-1-898910-11-4

13 Works of Plato V

Euthyphro, Meno, Protagoras, Theages, Laches, Lysis, Charmides, Lesser Hippias, Euthydemus, Hipparchus, Rivals, Menexenus, Clitopho, Io, Cratylus (together with virtually the whole of Proclus' Scholia), Epistles. An index to the extensive notes Taylor added to the 5 volumes. 978-1-898910-12-1

14 Apuleius' Golden Ass & Other Philosophical Writings

The Golden Ass (or Metamorphosis); On the Dæmon of Socrates; On the Philosophy of Plato. 978-1-898910-13-8

15 & 16 Proclus' Commentary on the Timæus of Plato

The Five Books of this Commentary in two volumes, with additional notes and short index. 978-1-898910-14-5 and 978-1-898910-15-2

17 Iamblichus on the Mysteries and Life of Pythagoras

Iamblichus On the Mysteries of the Egyptians, Chaldeans & Assyrians; Iamblichus' Life of Pythagoras; Fragments of the Ethical Writings of Pythagoreans; Political Fragments of Archytas, Charondas and other Pythagoreans. 978-1-898910-16-9

18 Essays and Fragments of Proclus

Providence, Fate and That Which is Within our Power; Ten Doubts concerning Providence; The Subsistence of Evil; The Life of Proclus; Fragments of Proclus' Writings. 978-1-898910-17-6

19 The Works of Aristotle I

The Physics, together with much of Simplicius' Commentary. A Glossary of Greek terms used by Aristotle. 978-1-898910-18-3

20 The Works of Aristotle II

The Organon: The Categories, On Interpretation, The Prior Analytics; The Posterior Analytics, The Topics, The Sophistical Elenchus; with extensive notes from the commentaries of Porphyry, Simplicius and Ammonius. 978-1-898910-19-0

21 The Works of Aristotle III

Great Ethics, Eudemian Ethics; Politics; Economics. 978-1-898910-20-6

22 The Works of Aristotle IV

Rhetorics; Nicomachean Ethics; Poetics. 978-1-898910-21-3

23 The Works of Aristotle V

The Metaphysics with extensive notes from the Commentaries of Alexander Aphrodisiensis and Syrianus; Against the Dogmas of Xenophanes, Zeno and Gorgias; Mechanical Problems; On the World; On Virtues and Vices; On Audibles. 978-1-898910-22-0

24 The Works of Aristotle VI

On the Soul (with much of the Commentary of Simplicius); On Sense and Sensibles; On Memory and Reminiscence; On Sleep and Wakefulness; On Dreams; On Divination by Sleep; On the Common Motions of Animals; On the Generation of Animals; On Length and Shortness of Life; On Youth and Old Age, Life and Death; On Respiration. 978-1-898910-23-7

25 The Works of Aristotle VII

On the Heavens (with much of the Commentary of Simplicius); On Generation and Corruption; On Meteors (with much of the Commentary of Olympiodorus). 978-1-898910-24-4

26 The Works of Aristotle VIII

History of Animals, & the Treatise on Physiognomy. 978-1-898910-25-1

27 The Works of Aristotle IX

The Parts of Animals; The Progressive Motions of Animals, The Problems; On Indivisible Lines. 978-1-898910-26-8

28 The Philosophy of Aristotle

Taylor's four part dissertation on the philosophy of Aristotle which outlines his primary teachings, the harmony of Plato and Aristotle, and modern misunderstandings of Aristotle. 978-1-898910-27-5

29 Proclus' Commentary on Euclid

Proclus' Commentary on the First Book of Euclid's Elements; Taylor's four part Dissertation on the Platonic Doctrine of Ideas, on Demonstrative Syllogism, On the Nature of the Soul, and on the True End of Geometry. 978-1-898910-28-2

30 The Theoretical Arithmetic of the Pythagoreans

The Theoretic Arithmetic of the Pythagoreans, Medicina Mentis, Nullities & Diverging Series, The Elements of a New Arithmetic Notation, Elements of True Arithmetic of Infinities. 978-1-898910-29-9

31 & 32 Pausanias' Guide to Greece

Pausanias' Guide to Greece (in two volumes) with illustrations and extensive notes on mythology. 978-1-898910-30-5 & 978-1-898910-31-2

33 Against the Christians and Other Writings

The Arguments of Julian Against the Christians; Celsus, Porphyry and Julian Against the Christians; Writings of Thomas Taylor from his Collectanea, his Miscellanies in Prose and Verse, and his short works On Critics, An Answer to Dr Gillies, A Vindication of the Rights of Brutes, and his articles from the Classical Journal. Included is a Thomas Taylor bibliography. 978-1-898910-32-9

Other titles available from the Prometheus Trust

Platonism and the World Crisis   John M Dillon, Brendan O'Byrne,
Tim Addey   978-1-898910-55-8

Towards the Noosphere   John M Dillon & Stephen R L Clark
                                            978-1-898910-60-2

Philosophy as a Rite of Rebirth – From Ancient Egypt to
Neoplatonism   Algis Uždavinys   978-1-898910-35-0

The Philosophy of Proclus – the Final Phase of Ancient Thought
L J Rosán   978 1 898910 44 2

The Seven Myths of the Soul   Tim Addey   978-1-898910-37-4

Release Thyself – Three Philosophic Dialogues Guy Wyndham-Jones
                                            978-1-898910-56-5

A Casting of Light by the Platonic Tradition Guy Wyndham Jones
                                            978-1-898910-57-2

The Song of Proclus – meditations from the Platonic Successor,
adapted by Guy Wyndham-Jones.   978-1-898910-62-6

An Index to Plato - A Subject Index using Stephanus pagination
                                            978-1-898910-34-3

The Iliad – Alexander Pope's Poetic translation of Homer's epic
                                            In preparation

The Odyssey – Alexander Pope's Poetic translation of Homer's epic
                                            In preparation

Students' Edition Paperbacks

The Symposium of Plato
Trans. Floyer Sydenham & Thomas Taylor. Includes Plotinus' On Love (En III, 5), and introductory essays.   978-1-898910-38-1

Know Thyself – The First Alcibiades & Commentary
Trans. Floyer Sydenham & Thomas Taylor, with introductory essays.
978-1-898910-39-8

Beyond the Shadows - The Metaphysics of the Platonic Tradition
Guy Wyndham-Jones and Tim Addey   978-1-898910-40-4

The Unfolding Wings - The Way of Perfection in the Platonic Tradition   Tim Addey   978-1-898910-41-1

The Sophist
Trans. Thomas Taylor, with introductory essays.   978-1-898910-93-0

The Meno
Trans. Floyer Sydenham & Thomas Taylor, with introductory essays.
978-1-898910-92-3

The Prometheus Trust is a registered UK charity. Apart from its publishing activities, it also offers education in philosophy, public lectures, workshops and conferences. Visit www.prometheustrust.co.uk